FEELING MATTERS

Books by Michael Eigen

Karnac Books

The Psychotic Core (1986, 2004)

The Electrified Tightrope (ed. Adam Phillips) (1993, 2004)

Psychic Deadness (1996, 2004)

Toxic Nourishment (1999)

Damaged Bonds (2001)

Other Publishers

Coming Through the Whirlwind (1992)

Reshaping the Self (1995)

The Psychoanalytic Mystic (1998)

Ecstasy (2001)

Rage (2002)

The Sensitive Self (2004)

Emotional Storm (2005)

Lust (2006)

FEELING MATTERS

From the Yosemite God to the Annihilated Self

Michael Eigen

KARNAC

First published in 2007 by
Karnac Books
118 Finchley Road, London NW3 5HT

Copyright © 2007 by Michael Eigen

The rights of the Contributors to be identified as the author of this work have been
asserted in accordance with §§ 77 and 78 of the Copyright Design and Patents Act
1988.

British Library Cataloguing in Publication Data

A C.I.P. for this book is available from the British Library

ISBN13: 978 1 85575 411 9
ISBN10: 1 85575 411 8

Edited, designed, and typeset by RefineCatch Ltd, Bungay, Suffolk
Printed in Great Britain

www.karnacbooks.com

Dedication

To a Better World

Which can not happen without more attention to experience and psychic life.

As long as feelings are second class citizens in public dialogue, people will be second class citizens.

Michael Eigen

Wounds hide in disbelief. We can't believe this happened, is happening, that such things can be. The traumatizing aspect of power counts on the time lapse between disbelief and horror, between the horror that leads to disbelief, and the horror that awakens realization of one's condition.

Election Rape (Chapter 5)

CONTENTS

CREDITS

CHAPTER TWO
Tiny Quivers. *Journal of Contemporary Psychoanalysis*, 42(1): 1–121 (2006). Reprinted with permission of The William Alanson White Institute.

CHAPTER FOUR
Trauma Clots. *POIESIS: A Journal of the Arts and Communication, VI* (May 2004).

CHAPTER SIX
Healing Longing in the Midst of Damage. *Psychoanalytic Dialogues, 15*(2): 169–183 (2005). Reprinted with permission of The Analytic Press.

CHAPTER NINE
Destruction and Madness, in J. Mills (Ed.) (2006). *Other Banalities: Melanie Klein Revisited*. London: Routledge.

CHAPTER TEN
The Annihilated Self. *The Psychoanalytic Review, 93*(1): 25–38 (2006). Reprinted with permission of the National Psychological Association for Psychoanalysis.

Introduction

D o books have desires? If so, the desire of this book is to add to the sum of human experience. It does so by small variations, a little like a piece by Philip Glass, or placing color slides on one another, or slowly rubbing joy and horror together.

Experience is an endangered species. It is getting flattened out and blown up, channeled with accelerating force through the will to profit. Profit and power set the tone for turning experience into sound bites, political hype or strategy, that at once excite and dull.

Education and the media can be added to religion as opiate of the masses. Political strategy shrinks experience into narrow bands of intensity (outrage, indignation) and plays on deeper helplessness, including loss of will or ability to think for oneself. I suppose it can be said that psychotherapy also shrinks experience. The word shrink spontaneously gravitated to therapists, who thought they were trying to expand human possibility. Politics and therapy *can* expand possibility but neither is without their areas of disaster.

A positive contribution therapy makes is to give people time. Yes, therapist and patient rush past each other or over each other, as is common in daily life. But an overall aim in therapy is to make time for experiencing, to give an ear to how people feel. Not to rush off after ten minutes because things are getting too complicated or uneasy. To stay with feelings building in the room, and stay some more. This is not how we usually interact in normal life and not doing so is one of the deficiencies that mark "normality". Psychotherapy is based on the premise that feelings matter and this book is dedicated to showing ways this is so. It does so not as dogma but as exploration, tentatively, for wherever we dip into experiential fields, more happens.

The therapist is not outside the emotional universe. No one is. It is not that the therapist removes herself from the emotional field. It is more that she is more used to working with it from within. It is an illusion to think we get "outside" our emotional life. Even if we are cold or dead, we are gripped by emotion. To be trapped by coldness or deadness is a powerful affective state. To *think* about emotion is not an unemotional business. It is permeated by a feeling perspective and passionate interest.

Now the truth: no one gets used to working with emotion from within. To work within emotional fields is always more than one can do. More truth: one is never up to the task. Psychically, we are babies trying to coordinate arms and legs before smooth coordination is possible. We flail along in semi-blundering fashion. There is the thrill of definite, worthwhile achievement. But this does not, can not, ought not end the way we feel before we locate or grasp that which excites us, before we can put it in our mouth.

Whether we are able to use or fathom it, there is one thing we can do, must do from the outset. We incessantly taste each other with eyes, bodies, thoughts, sensations. Psychic taste buds rarely rest. They feed us each other, gauge states of being, states of spirit. We taste each other's feeling tone and, in time, rightly or wrongly, sense background intentions.

This, then, is the desire of my book: to taste experiential possibilities, nuances, complexities, let them build and build some more. To try to sustain the growth of psychic taste buds, not play them down or pretend they don't exist. They *do* exist and permeate experience. A world tilted toward profit has little time for them, except to exploit them, make money out of them, convert them into the will to power.

One can not experience without suffering. New technologies to read brain images and change brain chemistry make it seem easier to control suffering. Proliferating use of medication makes one wonder what all this suffering is about. Who are we, where are we, and what are we doing, that such relief from our condition seems so necessary. It is unlikely medication will solve the human condition, although it helps many in distress. In the end, we have to work with each other, with ourselves. To grow psychic taste buds and digestive capacity in the face of suffering is our true evolutionary challenge.

I begin this book with a sense of silent awe in face of mute, ancient rocks (Chapter 1, "Yosemite God") and follow this awesome silence through dreamless sleep, profound void states in the background of our beings and their echoes in ethical awareness. The silent awe that ripples through our beings finds expression in such beautiful visions as Plato's Idea of the Good and Kant's reworking of the golden rule, to treat each other as ends rather than means.

Although the link I make between silent awe and ethical awareness is a crucial thread, life is more complex and quivering. In Chapter 2, "Tiny Quivers", a social woman, call her Kathryn, is married to a man who treasures solitude. They value each other but also are critical of one another, feeling each holds the other back. She bemoans the fact that therapies do not quite work for her. Something important starts to happen, then closes up, falls back. Or her therapist leaves, ending prematurely, as happened just before she saw me.

As time goes on two dramas emerge, one around social striving, the other more psychological, involving opening-closing. Kathryn wants to be a great success socially-professionally and is only a modest success. Much of her energy goes into making social contacts with an aim to bettering herself professionally. Her husband's stay-at-home attitude is an anchor, dragging her down yet stabilizing. She is very attractive, looks "normal", someone you'd want to be with. Except there is a kind of brittleness, sharpness, something closed. She is aware that she has a problem contacting herself. When feelings start to come, she closes off. It did not occur to her that this tendency to close down when feelings rise might play a role in closing off socially-professionally as well, her own hidden ceiling.

She tried to push past her cut off point in a way that felt thin, as if resources to support what she wanted had not yet arrived. She saw with her children that quality of responsiveness mattered, and began trying more with her husband. Little by little, therapy hinged on contacting ability to sustain contact, tiny emotional quivers moment to moment. One of her great fears: feelings would make her ugly, her trauma-free physiognomy would get messy, her mask of normalcy would crack and she did not know what would take its place.

Chapter 3, "Words", investigates relationships between words and wordlessness. The man at the center of this exploration, Harry, feels he is murdering people with his words, yet no one seems to know. People do not seem to feel the impact of his killer intentions, his killer words. He has the perception that people are always killing each other with words without awareness of what is going on.

Harry fantasizes himself as a baby in a state of heightened alertness, aware of anger dissolving because of its lack of impact. His anger missed its mark and circled back. Mute lack of impact stained his words. Words were like ants nibbling on a dumb, hostile immensity without sufficient effect. Something in his affect, and later affective speech, failed to find the Other.

Chapter 4, "Trauma Clots", explores complexities in a man, Arnie, who oversimplified his early life and paid a price for doing so. He kept telling himself his early life was easy and that was why life was too hard for him now. This little piece of idealization, based on gratifying aspects of reality, cloaked mixtures of delusion and realism that downplayed trauma. Psychoanalysis is criticized for making too much of trauma, worrying about early damage. Isn't life about resilience, getting on with it, sweeping past what stops you?

Creating delusional ideas about one's past means one is, in certain ways, living with delusion now. We are constituted in such a way that we make delusion sound like reality, part of everyday narrative, part of our picture of things. Sometimes therapy has a chance of helping people whose delusions begin to break down. At breakdown points, the impact of one's life has a chance of being felt. It is a ghastly property of the human that a person can go through life imagining its impact as not there. An impact-less life, life without impact: an impossibility, a hallucinated state, but not uncommon.

In Arnie's case, the contrast between myth and reality was stark. As therapy unfolded, trauma clots became visible, and inside these clots were such things as father's death, molestation in childhood, mother's psychosis (eventually she was permanently hospitalized), and self-created traumas to dramatize his condition. Arnie suffered intermittent breakdowns and in our first meeting announced his determination to kill himself if therapy did not work. This is scary enough in any circumstance, but scarier as I understood he meant, if therapy did not fulfill the idealized mythos of his childhood. It was imperative to see that life was never trauma free.

The playing down of trauma can have disastrous consequences. The Bush administration played down the trauma of war in its rush to war with Iraq. They depicted initial bombings ("shock and awe", trauma terms treated like wondrous fireworks) in a way that softened experiencing real impact. Waves of idealization of process and goal dulled the sense that lives were lost and twisted out of shape, that lies twisted the country out of shape. It's awful to see trauma idealized in individual lives and social policy. Idealization blunts traumatic impacts. The latter often build, multiplying devastation, before awakening realization. To blunt the pain one causes is part of traumatic artfulness. Self-exoneration is part of the will to power.

Delusion is part of individual and group processes, part of the way our minds work. We can not free ourselves of delusion but at least we can be aware that we are delusional beings. This awareness might, at least, slow down our zeal for destructive action offered as "solutions" to problems.

Chapter 5, "Election Rape", knits individual and social problems together. Carla, my patient, speaks of election rape and graphically describes feeling violated by George W. Bush's election as president in 2000. Violation on the public scene linked up with violation in her family, from infancy on, so that she read one in the other. Reverberations between the most intimate areas of self and group atmosphere and action are more pervasive and telling than is ordinarily realized. Personal, familial, and public domains permeate and penetrate each other in ways that often escape attention.

Chapter 6, "Healing Longing in the Midst of Damage", focuses on a woman's sense of damage. The person she was most attached to and most trusted, her therapist, stopped seeing her, leaving her in excruciating pain. She went from therapist to therapist without being able to start another relationship. I, too, was unable to see her, but we met intermittently. A lot happened in sporadic meetings.

A sense grew that she needed to live out damaged attachment and loss. Intensity of injury was important, addictive perhaps, and more than addictive. It was a kind of emotional nourishment, quasi-toxic nourishment, a piercing agony that both filled and emptied her spirit (Eigen, 1999, 2001). Without it, anxiety was unbearable. With it, anxiety was nearly unbearable.

She discovered in my office a paper by another analyst (Ghent, 1990) who wrote about the importance of "surrender", a giving oneself to life, not holding back. She idealized this bit of goodness as an antidote to clinging, but felt she could never give herself to such an experience. It might be possible for others but not for her. She was too damaged, a lost cause. Yet . . .

Chapter 7, "Alone Points", touches a place in me that can not speak, a stuck point I do not seem to be able to move out of. When I am in that place, I am unable to respond if a patient wants more from me. If I am responding, I am unable to communicate it. Whatever I communicate is not satisfactory. The patient's desire falls flat, hits a wall. She loses, for the time, my emotional support.

Others have this silent spot as well. Sometimes emotional fullness makes us quiet. But what concerns me in this chapter is a freeze, a profound immobility, an inability, muteness that does not budge. The person across from me can be shouting, "Fire!" but a dull glare of mute immobility, uncomfortable and apologetic, stares back.

Rage is one way to break immobility, or try to. In Chapter 8, "Filling Up With Rage", the rage propensity of three individuals is explored. Aspects of rages that are detailed include filling the self with feeling, humiliation of self and other, momentary sense of god-like totality, fusion of entitlement and self-righteousness with a sense of justice and violation, and a haunting sense of inability to feel one's impact. Phrases like impotent or helpless rage strike a deep chord, expressive of dynamics of immobility and helplessness, a failure of ability to contact and feel the effect of one's actions on others. In many individuals, such an inability is rooted in growing up in an emotional void, where sensitivity to mutual impact is damaged. Often, society teaches that it is more profitable to ignore how we affect each other, except as it pertains to getting ahead, winning, or striking back when loss and humiliation threaten. High volume rage blots out inability and deficit, whether on personal, emotional or larger societal levels. The quiet of therapy provides a hearing for a wider range of personal responsiveness, space for psychic nutrients very much needed.

Chapter 9, "Boxes of Madness", is the most "technical" or "theoretical" chapter of this book. It focuses on aspects of Melanie Klein's work, and concludes with use of D. W. Winnicott and Jacques Lacan in this discussion. Klein is my focus because she puts madness and destructiveness squarely at the center of her vision. She gives a detailed account of mad dynamics in human life, linked with what she calls "the destructive urge within". She explores madness and destructiveness related to self, others, environment and world. It was largely her work that marked a shift in psychoanalysis to see neurosis as a defense against psychotic anxieties. The great work of Winnicott (1992) and Bion (1992) so concerned with vicissitudes of madness, followed.

For years, her work was discredited because of her use of Freud's death drive, a questionable concept. However one takes her use of this notion, the importance of annihilation anxiety and its relationship with psychotic and psychopathic destructiveness has been born out by war, human injury, and the melding of economic, political, and technological hubris (if not megalomania). Klein's (1946; 1957) emphasis on a double nucleus in the human psyche, a good core and destructive gradient, or as she puts it in one of her book titles, gratitude and envy, has much to teach us today. At a minimum, it is a signal, an alert, an alarum. The work of destruction is double directional, at once fuelling a sense of power, yet leading to ennui, depletion, a dread of having no impact, leaving one impotent and unreal.

The book ends with portrayals of the way self dies while we are alive (Chapter 10, "The Annihilated Self"). We carry with us annihilated corners of our beings. For many they are not corners, but something central. Annihilation varies from pockets we try not to notice to soul murder that must be addressed.

Health is a broad term with many dark threads. Some brands of health feed off annihilated aspects of others. To meet and come to grips with the annihilated self is a major task of society. Social forces play off unconscious areas of annihilation, exploit it, titillate and irritate it, scapegoat it. A leader, thinking himself healthy, may be driven to exhibit inner deformity by deforming others. He may even need war – the horror of injury and annihilation – to feel clean and right. Leaders often express forces at work in groups.

We have come a long way from the silent awe at Yosemite to silence that kills. A very positive feeling threads its way through this book, a love of life, an affirmation. Yet as we wade in more deeply, we discover ways in which our impact on life is not registered or felt. A sense of helplessness and impotence in face of awesome forces increases. We put a tracer on this thread, the sense of no or little impact, as we move through chapters. The annihilated self is a more extreme instance of this tendency, but it is not uncommon.

FEELING MATTERS
From the Yosemite God to the
Annihilated Self

CHAPTER ONE

Yosemite God[1]

Yosemite silenced me. Words dissolved. A wordless world for millions of years. What can speaking do? Tears, awe, like so many other people before me. Mammoth rocks, mammoth stars. God's beauty. The soul of the rock says, "Come closer."

A sign says, "Here is where Theodore Roosevelt camped with John Muir, spoke good forest talk, and left Roosevelt inspired to conserve remnants of nature's forests and wilderness."

So this is what words can do – inspire great thoughts, feelings, actions. In people so different as Theodore Roosevelt and myself, words can and do make a difference.

What I put into my writings, my books: words that echo the silence, the wind and water – the spirit that hovers, runs through, uplifts, dashes down.

Not God as signifier for inbuilt, unknown intelligence. But God that gives birth to religions. Religions that reveal and obscure. Religions that botch it but provide hints, openings, pointers, God-prints. I would not go so far as to say that religions are God fossils in which God is embedded without life. Religions can and do help implant God in us, awaken us, get us going to some extent, in some ways. Are they necessary? Can't Yosemite do it alone? Doesn't Yosemite ignite the God sense all by itself? Doesn't Yosemite ignite God? Surely, God, too, must be awed, dumbfounded, amazed, moved, swept away, by forms creation takes.

Look at what words do, their danger. I said religions help implant God, as if God were an implant, a graft, a foreign organ. As if religions put into us what they grow out of and express. Maybe we should take religions more as a gush, an outcry, a moan, a whisper, an unfolding prayer. Like the last psalms, shouts of joy, banging cymbals, blowing horns, King David's dancing, singing. Songs that echo what life feels like when aliveness quivers and surges.

Yet religions *are* God implants. Lighting shabbos candles, eating chalah, learning that rest is very special, very holy, more holy even than repentance. My Hebrew school teacher was fond of shocking us by saying, Shabbos, the sabbath, is holier than Yom Kippur, the Day of Atonement. On shabbos we can even rest from repenting. You have your childhood memories, your implants. And when they work, these plants grow and grow and you grow with them and the holy grows too.

Often they do not work well, they mar, deform. We try to pull them out of us, run away, take another route. We run and run. Some of us – many here – run to psychoanalysis. We run to psychoanalysis to save us from God, a bad implant. Often we call these implants parents.

It can be difficult to distinguish good from bad, toxins from nourishment, undamaged from damage. Few things are more binding, more gripping than toxic nourishment and damaged bonds. The way God is stuffed into us by the religious often poisons the spirit, damages the soul. We use psychoanalysis, in part, to pump out our psychic stomachs and restore ability to digest experience.

Some criticize psychoanalysis for teaching people to tolerate toxins. Others see a truer calling, to work with poisons and damage, to approach what we fear, to come closer to challenging our makeup. Psychoanalysis is less a medicine than an act of creation, an incessant shaping, re-texturing, fine tuning of affective attitudes.

The God I know wants us to create, to taste the power that makes us giddy. Giddy with God, harmless with others. To be harmless with others – something that will never happen. Does God want us to practice the art of something that will never happen? For example, to achieve a world without murder?

We created psychoanalysis to re-create ourselves. If not to re-create ourselves, at least to try to help ourselves, or at least to work with ourselves. I say we, but of course I mean Freud. But once a tool leaves its maker's hand anyone can make use of it. And there is no telling to what uses it may be put. For example, Marx and Lenin's depiction of historical forces, expressed in communism. An attempt to help ourselves, to cure society, to make a fairer life. But things we do to help ourselves turn out to be mixed blessings, if blessings at all.

If I were making a movie, we would eavesdrop on God telling heavenly hosts, "Let's send them Freud and psychoanalysis with the hope they'll do a better job working with their impulses." God tried a lot of ways before without enormous success. Floods and plagues didn't work. Neither did abusive, punitive religions promising heaven for behaving and hell for being bad. We've been very bad children. We just don't act very well. So here comes psychoanalysis to take another shot at it. Working with impulses in a freer, indirect way. With free association and free floating attention: saying whatever you want, listening in new ways. Perhaps psychoanalysis wants to teach us how to be bad in a better way, a less destructive way.

As we worked with this new toy – professionals called it a method – we found that much more than impulse control was at stake. Fields of intertwining, pulsing, rigid and shifting affective attitudes swam into view. We found not just caesuras, blinks, and fissures of consciousness through which we thought we glimpsed work of unconscious processes. More and more, focus turned to nuances of emotional transmissions, dialectics of permeability and evacuation, how we take in and get rid of ourselves and others. How quality of unconscious processing of emotional life affects quality of existence, as well as the reverse. Less sticks and carrots than opening fields of experience.

Awareness of the importance of dream-work grew. Winnicott (1992) felt dreaming contributes to the use of experience, making life feel real. Bion connects dream-work to processing emotional experience. We have to dream life into reality. Damaged dream-work leaves us in a state of chronic emotional indigestion or shut down. For Bion (1992; Eigen, 2001) something like dream-work goes on day and night, linking levels and forms of existence, taking life in, working it over, giving back in profound interweaving.

But there is, too, experience beyond dreaming. Dreaming is already on the road to narrative structures and rationalizations we can work with while awake. We sleep not only to dream, but to allow contact with places dreaming can't reach, that reach towards dreaming. Bion (1992: 149–50) suggests one reason sleep is essential is to make possible emotional experiences the personality can not have while awake. Sleep enables experience outside the reach of waking and dreaming to move towards dreaming's reach.

This idea coheres with the Hindu saying that everyday life is the past, dreaming is the present, and dreamless void the future.

Shall we call this a wordless, imageless unconscious, a portal through which our lives are fed impalpably and ineffably by experience that accesses us in dreamless sleep? As though God or nature or evolution has safeguarded something from our use of it, a special form of contact that we can not ruin with our controlling narratives or our lust for power or our fears. That gains access to us when our ordinary focus and selective attention, even the foci of our dreams, are out of play. A contact that accesses us when we're not looking.

Yet there are threads in waking life that reverberate with the ineffable background of our beings. The thunderous silence of Yosemite, a wordless awe, feels connected to the impalpable portal in dreamless sleep that freshens life. There are words that come from this contact too, however much they obscure it. "Hear O Israel, the Lord is God, the Lord is One." It is an accident of language that "hear" and "here" sound the same, and that God's name might translate as, "I am here." Soundless hearing, a here-ing, an ingredient of dreamless contact through which experience closed by personality finds openings. Yosemite, then, touches us because it is so old yet stimulates an awesome sense of replenishment, eternal replenishment, that goes on in our sleep.

Would it be too much to suggest that something of our ethical sense is fed by dreamless sleep? A taste of peace, refreshment, replenishment. New possibilities of experiencing entering, given a chance to touch us through sleep. How can something touch us if we are not aware of it? An aporia that marks our existence, our plasticity.

Perhaps marks us with a sense of mystery.

The peace found in dreamless sleep gives us something most dreams can not provide. It takes us deeper than conflict, antagonism, fear. So many dreams have persecutory elements, distilling and exaggerating frictions of waking life. Where does the idea of peace come from? One source, I feel, is the profundity of sleep. The association of "profound" with sleep is no accident. That sleep can be profound gifts us with a profound sense of peace that daily anxieties can not exhaust. A peace we may fail to access while awake but which enters while we're asleep. We look forward to sleep after a day of activity, not just to refresh ourselves, but to contact the deep peace that rest and sleeping can bring. A peace we may consciously try to base ourselves on through prayer and meditation.

Sleep is not peaceful for everyone. Damage can be so profound or consciousness so heightened and vigilant, that sleep is difficult. Many complain of not being able to let go, surrender, give themselves to sleep. For some, sleep is murderous and dreams are often nightmares. The traumatic background of our beings has free reign in sleep. Even so, many for whom sleep is fearsome treasure peaceful moments that sneak through, moments when sleep overtakes them and profound peace seeps in. After waking, the message is garbled. Terror as usual reigns. A person may express regret, grief or anger that peace does not last longer. Memory of it remains, if nearly obliterated, and one wants more of it.

Some people for whom sleep is too twisted for much peace find heightened moments of meaning while awake. A beautiful color sky, tree, hill, a painting, a facial expression, tone of voice, a kind gesture, music: a taste of the Yosemite God and the impalpable background of being breaks through and raises existence. A flash of insight, reading, writing and insomnia pays off. A kind of peace is part of heightened awareness, even if awareness shatters. A bit like the peace of fireworks, the lighting up, incandescence, shattering and fall.

An awesome peace, stirring in Yosemite grandeur. A stirring peace embedded in heights of awakening and depths of sleep. There are, then, different kinds of peace. I am interested in an enlivening one. Peace that stirs, lifts. It is not just that I am little and Yosemite is big, or that we are both changing and passing, slowly or quickly. We are both amazing in spirit, the great spirit of the rock, my thrilling awareness of the rock, a stirred and stirring awareness. Coming alive, shivering by being touched by, invaded by stone. A grandeur that transfers to ordinary experience, that is part of the touch of flesh.

There are great ideas that link with this profound stirring. For me,

Plato's vision of the Good is one, Kant's treating each other as ends, not just means, is another. These ideas link with the golden rule, giving, caring, putting oneself in the place of the other. Kant speaks of the moral universe as more thrilling than the starry skies. Where does the idea of peace, of caring, treating others as ends come from in a world permeated by survival needs, practicality, antagonisms, lust for power?

A vision of natural divisions vs. strife is one possibility: Taoism vs. Empedocles or Heraclitus perhaps. Some speak of dialectics, paradox, the contribution of diverse tendencies and tensions to a greater whole. Emmanuel Levinas (1969; Eigen, 2005) draws on another possibility, expressed in our response to the human face. An ethical sense inscribed in our flesh, growing through our experience of the Other, particularly another's expressive face.

Levinas writes of a vulnerability, an infinite appeal, even a destitution. The other calls for our response. We are not speaking of the other as master now, or slave, but the other as naked before God, as naked to others, needy, yes, but also at risk. We all ask something of others and it is that something we are all required to give. An infinite asking, an infinite giving. Neither term can be exhausted.

An enfleshed infinite, an immediate infinite, infinite immediacy: from an infant's response to its mother's face, to our response as grownups to each other. An infinite immediacy that embraces, that upholds within it as its nucleus an infinite distance, intimate distance that calls for respect as well as caring. To see and sense as a form of giving. How can distance be an infinite immediacy, an inexhaustible caring? Doesn't distance run the range from cruel to compassionate? To live a difference that does justice to what is lived: isn't this an immediacy worth striving for?

We have had time to learn how injury is inflicted, to read the pain we create in one before us. To behead the enemy, the stranger, to destroy the intimate: we know these well. We are an abusive species, a tormented species, a pain inflicting group.

We know how defensive we are, warding off the pain that is our heritage, that comes at us from all directions. We know, too, what it is like to support life in one in need. To come through ourselves, to help. Have we decided as a group which is the greater satisfaction, the greater prompting? Have we decided to water down the appeal – a mutual appeal – that brings life to another level?

Which do we imagine the greater fear: that we will be empty if not brutal, or empty if not giving? We dread losing either way, as if we need both to feel alive, a dependency, an addiction to the dialectics of brutality and giving. Part of suicide bombing's compelling genius is that both poles maximally combine: the flash of brutality and fullness of self-giving. Giving oneself to God or cause, supported in the background by devoted faces, friends, mother, militant brothers. The flaw: to believe some faces are human, some are not.

What Levinas speaks of is the appeal of faces everywhere, universal appeal, a concrete universal embedded in experience. An immediate appeal that experience is made of. No exclusions. This is the ethical aim inscribed in our looking, hearing, feeling bodies, the aim that lifts us, impels us into life beyond murder. An impossibility, perhaps. But when we sense it we know that Kant is right, it is a beauty the stars themselves sing to. A happening that brings a smile to every infant's heart and face, a spontaneous smile in response to another, alive with expressive, touching radiance – unless something has gone horribly wrong.

What, then, are we called on to give? We are asked to give ourselves. To give of ourselves. And for this, no one else will do. There are no substitutes for what only you bring now, this particular, passing forever.

A patient, call him Cusp, dreams of sex with a pretty girl beyond his reach. He is fearful. Did something happen? Tallish girl. He also dreams of giving a seminar, a talk. There is a water sound in the background, pleasant enough, perhaps a distraction. Should he shut the doors, windows?

The next week he does give a weekend seminar in the country for a well known group and sleeps with someone he meets there. A tallish girl beyond his reach he normally would be fearful of approaching. In the country seminar setting, they readily fell in with each other, but only for a single night. The next day she was already bobbing in the sea of events, moving away from him, free spirit. She touched him with her magic wand and he felt renewed, redeemed, gulping loss as part of the richness.

Sex as a redemptive act. Redeemed through a moment's contact with another person, with her body, being allowed entrance, being held, smiled at, felt. A good moment that won't solve daily problems or particular torments, that won't makeover a wounded self. Merely a passing forever that adds light in the background of being and a sense of being worthy. It is not the first time he felt it.

He asks if everyone sees Light during sex.

I don't know about everyone but I often do. I don't think I did at first. I suspect, at first, I felt I was getting away with something, that sex was taboo, a sense of triumph part of the thrill. But by the time I was moving out of my twenties, definitely in my early thirties, light was a regular visitor, in the darkness in and around my head, behind my eyes, trickling through skin, surges beneath and within and over my body, my incorporeal corporeal body. It streams from my partner's face, lighting the room. In a semi-comic way, Keith Herring expresses this by lines representing light pulses around penises. Sensation glows. Feeling glows. You sometimes see this glow in animals.

Keith Herring's penis glows are real, as are halos around the heads of angels and saints in medieval and renaissance paintings. Such representations can also be misleading. They are so highly localized, whereas the light my patient and I experience is hard to pin down. It is part of what gives rise to notions of spirit being everywhere. But I would have to add, to be true to my experience, more densely packed here and there, undulating, fluid, with varying concentrations, yet also glowing with undying, golden intensity, an uplifting thrill with no beginning or end, even when ignited by sex organs. I have had similar experience in many places, many forms.

For example, I felt God more highly concentrated in Jerusalem than other places I visited. The golden illumination seemed to be part of the dry land, the old walls, the light. God was in the land, the air. Inner-outer luminous sensation, ineffable sensation. Perhaps sensation *is* ineffable. A lighting, heightening, awakening that the region's bitter pain fails to disconfirm. God is infinitely everywhere, but there are infinite fluctuations in infinity. This coheres with shifting numinous densities that characterize the influence of ancient gods on changing fortunes. Freud distilled such experience in his notion of libido, energy expressed by liquid and electrical images, changing forms and densities, instantaneously distributed from place to place. A sexual cosmic vision, after all.

If spirit affects environment and environment affects spirit, I fear what evil in the land does to the air of Washington, D.C. There is good too, always a struggle between good and evil, although we differ in saying which is which. A sense of wanting to do right by life, to do justice to life and each other, remains alive through remnants,[2] as the Bible says. Nevertheless, life is sacrificed over differing definitions of justice, or perversions of justice, a horribly apt phrase.

We seem to have drifted downstream from Cusp's dream. As we may expect, double currents make up the dream, opening and closing, on the analogue of pulsation, Lacan's (1978, pp. 32, 125, 143) image for the opening and closing of the unconscious. To open, to close. A basic rhythm. The dream movement also involves approaching the unapproachable, touching the untouchable, which Cusp tastes in dream and waking life.

The contrast between dream and waking life is porous. Dreaming is a kind of waking life that goes on while sleeping and something akin to dreaming goes on while we are awake. Dreaming and waking converge to give Cusp a sense of reaching the unreachable. A taste of sexual grace. It is a feeling we treasure. It makes life feel worthwhile. It is a grace and a challenge that percolates in the background of our being. Perhaps enough good experiences (can there be enough?) summate past a critical point and create a better imbalance. For much of life, a little good goes a long way.

Part of the joy in sexual grace is the goodness that flows through maimed and strangulated areas of self. Love or pleasure or possibility touches a monster within. A heart smile, for the moment, redeems grotesque, deformed elements of body and soul, a little like beauty and the beast. We feel ourselves touched by goodness, even feel ourselves good.

The challenge is the time and work that go into encoding goodness into daily living. Can goodness survive our lives? Inform our lives? It is one thing to enjoy a blessed night in dream or flesh. Another to bring goodness into the world, to mediate good births, to incarnate goodness in daily living. Good people have tried a long time to make goodness count. To a certain extent, they succeed, even as life sweeps much of their efforts away. To a certain extent, we are stymied, since the will to do good often harms.

The Bible documents not just lust for life and the struggle for existence. But the struggle of goodness to survive, to make life better, the ever besieged need to treat each other in better ways. The Bible sets goals, like "do not kill each other", but does not show us the way. Even God gets exasperated and tries to wipe us out. We survive like ants eating crumbs of mercy slipping through fits of rage. We are a scandal, a shame, an outrage. But we pick ourselves up and light shines through us. Not just at night in bed, but at this meeting today in broad daylight, in our discourse, in our hopes.

No one has the answers. We can not tell ahead of time what the outcome of decisions or actions will be. We need many kinds of contributions, science, art, politics, all walks of life. I do feel psychoanalysis adds something to the brew. In psychoanalysis we learn a little more about destruction. We learn or think we learn that feelings matter, that we are sensitive beings who need to sense how sensitivity works, that ethics has roots in sensitivity to ourselves and others. Psychoanalysis does not have the answers either but provides avenues for exploring new forms of dialogue, new probes, new ventures of spirit. It, at least, highlights difficulties and challenges our enigmatic, packed psyche brings.

We are not transparent to ourselves or others, although we like to think so. We see things others hide from themselves and they see things we hide. But that does not make seeing omniscient, profound or helpful. It is not what we see but how we use what we see that aids or harms quality of living.

Antagonism is everywhere. At boundaries between groups and individuals, in families, nations, within the self. A certain antagonism is part of our psychic immune system. As Kant has it, we're a sort of unsocial social group. Our protective hostility easily runs amok, like fantasy porcupines inflicting injury while trying to keep warm.

And yet there is a seed of unquenchable optimism in our sea of pessimistic realism. Aren't we catching on that it is up to us to work with the equipment we have been given, to partner our capacities, not just exploit them, to learn and keeping learning about our make-up? Isn't that what we have been trying to do for thousands of years, probably longer? Isn't that where evolution is taking us – closer to opposing our need to murder (whether physical, economic, social, or spiritual)? Closer to embracing struggle with our make-up and trying to do better?

Psychoanalysis is one attempt to see what we can do if we open more boxes, combining models of control with models of affective exploration and emotional transmission. Whatever its limitations and failures, psychoanalysis addresses aspects of psychic reality that must be grappled with. Attempts to outlaw or ban the psyche – by science, spirit, laughter, or shouting – delay the work that has to be done. Work unknown. We can not bully the psyche out of existence.

We glimpse ways of being together that I don't think quite existed before. Ways of feeling each other, exercising emotional taste buds, modes of relating that encompass but are more interesting than beating each other down. A cutting edge of evolution involves what it is like for people to be together. Affective attitude is a raw material shaping us as we shape it, creating richly textured possibilities of being. To listen, sense and speak: a long journey ahead, no less important than reshaping colors, material forms, genes and neural chemicals. Evolution of hearing, sensing, speaking: evolution materiality now depends on. Our sense of value and self-esteem depend on this evolution.

Kant contrasts self-esteem and well-being. To evolve towards life in which we affirm one another's worth – infinite worth – entails sacrifice of well-being, ease, inertia. True self-esteem depends on it. I want to close this chapter with a saying by Kant to reflect on: "Nature is utterly unconcerned that man live well, only that he bring himself to the point where his conduct makes him worthy of life and well-being" (p. 31). When we think of spirituality, let us not omit this consideration.

Notes

1. Yosemite refers to Yosemite National Park in California. This chapter grows from my visit there in the summer of 2004. Its rock formations are awesome.
2. The Bible frequently refers to a good remnant that remains after God's destructive spasms and rampages. This refers to survival or triumph of good over evil in the end. Yet it is also an experience traversed over and over. A prototype is Noah's survival after the flood, and is an image that threads its way through many biblical tales, pronouncements, songs and prayers. In *Human Nature* (1988, p. 76), Winnicott's diagrams of internal good and bad objects give plurality to the latter, but a little good goes a long way.

CHAPTER TWO

Tiny Quivers

athryn asked if I trained with "X-School" because I used the
word *contact* at our last meeting. At *that* meeting she was
warm and weepy and somewhat fearful. Inner tremolo,
body quivering, a tiny bit open.

Open vs. closed was a theme of the last session. Kathryn spoke
tearfully about losing her analyst, who stopped treatment to have a
baby. After having her baby, the woman decided to take an indefin-
ite break from practice. Two months, four months, six months – now
a year, no end in sight. Kathryn was at a loss. Her analyst was very
special.

She consulted several therapists in the interim. They were helpful
but did not possess that special something – a tone, quality of being
that made Kathryn feel seen and heard through and through. The
consultants understood this or that and struck a balance between
support and challenge. Kathryn could get along with them. But that
special something was missing. Kathryn felt the limits of the treatment as it happened, hitting the other's sharp places, having to pull
back into herself, show only certain areas. The people she met were
good at what they did but somehow missed the whole person.

I molded myself to the moment as best I could but sensed the effort I made to be a little warmer, fuller, open. I knew her past analyst and knew she was kindly, astute, more light of touch, spontaneously gentle than I. I felt rougher, cruder, more relentless, visionary, mythic. I have some special qualities, a special sensitivity to mood, affect quivers, quality of facial expressions, imagery, tone of being and bearing, my own way of sensing the life of the whole. I can get lost in processes, semi-dose, not be there enough or be too jagged, uneven, awkward, out of whack, out of sync. The natural balance of qualities that Kathryn experienced with her last analyst, she might not find with me. Some people find it freeing to be with me, and Kathryn might too, but I'm not sure she'd feel so thoroughly recognized and responded to as she did with the woman who left her.

She was angry that she was a working mother and her analyst stopped working to be a full time mother. It was part of Kathryn's ideology, as well as desire, to do both. She felt betrayed that her analyst would choose one or the other, and that home life took precedence. A regressive choice, she felt, a retreat from feminism, an indulgence. It was difficult to take in that her analyst felt her baby more important than her work. The good maternal presence Kathryn was lucky to taste with her analyst found a real baby enough for now.

D. W. Winnicott (1965: 52–4, 85–6) speaks of the "primary maternal preoccupation" the mother goes through, a period in the first months of the infant's life when the mother is nearly fully absorbed in caring for her baby. Attunement approaches perfection, as the mother tries to sense the baby's needs and fill them. Gradually, she comes to herself, the spell somewhat broken, and she wakes to life outside her baby. The fullness of devotion spontaneously modulates to fit the baby's developmental movement. Even in the midst of primary maternal absorption, Winnicott's mother has a certain mindful percipience, intuitively sensing the infant's own reality, so that mother love is not simply blind. To a certain extent, her and the baby's need for more outside their relationship grows together.

I suspect that a grain of primary maternal preoccupation informs the whole of therapy and is part of an empathic current that flows through life. It plays a role in the sense of injury our sensitivity is prone to. Sometimes growth tendencies try to break free of this empathic underpinning, feeling imprisoned by the latter. The empathic grounding of our lives, sweet as it is, can be felt as suffocating, and we seek fresh air.

Therapy, too, embraces conflicting tendencies and does its best with them. Therapy break-ups play a role in this process. Loss and break-up is as much a part of therapy as feeling connected. This fact or possibility gets obscured by accidental loss, acts of fate, contingencies, the therapist moving, dying, changes of circumstance. In the case of Kathryn's therapist, becoming a mother.

Wounded sensitivity is a fact of experience. How it comes about, what it means, what is done with it, varies. Kathryn warms to therapy and begins to open, and her therapist leaves. Everything is surrounded by good reasons, good intentions. Yet rupture occurs. Attempts to rationalize it are somewhat ameliorating, but loss and pain persist. Kathryn fears closing up again. She feels herself becoming rigid, shutting down, not as bad as she once was, but not where she wants to be. She feels her gains in danger and searches for someone to open with. She goes from therapist to therapist, looking for an opener. People do this with jobs, sexual partners, interests. Writers and artists live it out going from book to book, painting to painting, a productive way to relish many creativity partners. Kathryn channels it in therapy. She does not want loss to ruin her chance to open.

I was not surprised to see her pulling back. That we had a good session made her wary. What if I was not the right therapy partner? What if she gave herself to the process and I failed her? It was precisely a good session that aroused more anxiety, since more was at stake. At that session she expressed anger at her past analyst and a host of other emotions, fear, grief, worry. A rich swirl of feelings. She confessed that she sat on her anger with her therapist, fearful of breaking the attunement she valued. This was the closest she ever came to the rage she knew she felt, rage at many things, including being confined by the goodness that helped her open.

In the past, anger had been part of closing. She hadn't reached the place where it could be part of a deeper opening. It was not that she was a goody-goody. She had gone through angry rebellion, angry expression of difference, angry affirmation, angry assertion of rights. It was not that anger was foreign to her. Anger made her life better but at a price. She felt herself constricting around it, molding to it, a kind of inner hardening, tight, angular, squeezed. She was grateful to her analyst for enabling a deeper opening but they never got to a place where anger became a natural part of the mix.

She suspects her analyst did not like to deal with anger but she never got the chance to find out. Kathryn wants to reach a more inclusive openness, to go farther, but fears failure. She fears gains slipping away, life slipping away, although she is in a better place than she used to be. She now knows, really knows, quality of responsiveness matters. She sees the difference with her children as well as herself. When feelings flow, things go better. When tightness comes, tumult heads towards disaster. Even walking down a street – sunlight is alive when she is alive. When the walls and dead zone come and she is a metal fist, sun cools, does not support life. How open can one be when fists are needed? You might say her analysis aborted when her analyst gave birth, but she tasted a responsiveness that gives deeper value to life. The fact that responsiveness has limits does not diminish its value, although Kathryn has a hard time with this asymmetry.

In the gap between sessions, she moved from responsiveness to rigidity, not uncommon in itself. But I was startled by her associating the word *contact* with a particular analytic school. I used the word contact when she spoke of her fear that she would come out and be left dangling, that I would not respond, that I'd emotionally vanish if she got into working with me. I remember saying something along the line that she could let me know if she felt I was out of contact or not in contact enough. She could somehow signal that things are taking a wrong turn. I can make adjustments, be more or less there as needed. She can play a role in signaling contact needs.

I felt something wrong when I made that remark. It was near the end of the session and there was no time to find out what happened. I had no idea that *contact* was a buzz word for her, a signifier of loss of connection, unresponsiveness, triggering dread of emotional starvation. My sense that something went wrong faded into the background, since much seemed to go right. Something wrong doesn't go away and in Kathryn's case it mobilized fright and flight and fight. When I saw her next time, I felt an electrified grid.

"Are you a member of X-School? Did you train with them?"

"I spent time with them years ago and found them helpful."

"I was in analysis with one of them. The theory was you wait for the patient to reach for contact, a sort of demand feed orientation. If the analyst does not think the patient is seeking contact, he remains silent. The patient is rewarded for attempts to make contact and does not get over-stimulated. I nearly starved to death. I couldn't take it. You were supposed to put your anger into words or discover how you couldn't, how it worked on you inside. I ended feeling stranded, alone and miserable. I hated the angry isolation his ungivingness left me with. Every time I screwed up courage to leave, he talked about my resistance to getting better. When you told me I could try to contact you, I thought you were one of them."

I was dumbfounded. The word contact meant such different things to each of us. To her it meant failure, incapacity, painful isolation. To me it meant life, including life's difficulties: difficulties involved in making contact and difficulties contact brings. Difficulty and richness.

A moment's reflection opened depths of problems. A penumbra of lack of contact clings to the word contact, otherwise why speak of making contact? To make contact implies states in which contact is not made, where barriers or impediments exist. One is more or less in or out of contact at a particular time (t). One might be more in contact with x, less in contact with y, and this may vary or reverse at t_1, t_2, t_3 . . ., where any t contains, enfolds, relates to many t's and where x and y may be psychic states, dimensions, regions of being, between or within individuals. I might feel painfully out of contact, while Kathryn might be in contact (with aspects of self, other, life), or vice versa, many shadings. Lack of contact can be part of a natural subsiding, gliding away, a mini-vacation from relating, or it can involve chronic disability.

In discussing a case, W. R. Bion (1992: 143) remarks, "Well, either this means that in my view and with my personality it is impossible to have any but the most tenuous contact with someone, or that for some reason much fuss is being made about an experience – contact with another – which is quite ordinary and taken by most people in their stride."

Bion may have had difficulty with contact and, if so, it is a relief to hear him say so or, at least, allude to it. He goes on to point out difficulties adhering to experience of contact and speaking of such. What is taken for granted in ordinary life is broken down in analysis. But the problem is deeper, inasmuch as breakdowns of people in ordinary life bring problems with contact in their wake. It is not just that analysis destroys what ordinary life takes for granted, but that destruction in ordinary life, including destruction of personality, drives analysis to seek and develop languages of breakdown and contact more capable of doing justice to these facts.

Freud proposed a link between libido and interest. Withdrawal of libido and interest from the outside world go together, as do investment of libido and interest. Libido may be withdrawn from the outside world and invested in the I. But it may also be withdrawn from the I, as one becomes increasingly depleted and out of contact, so that life, others, and oneself become more and more unreal. Freud (1911) saw in psychotic hallucination an attempt to restore relations between self and other: restoration of lost reality in a hallucinated key. Schreber, for example, describes a "blackout" in which the world ends – a caesura in which self ends as well – then is "miracled up" again in hallucinated and delusional ways.

Schreber's breakdowns followed professional success and loss of loved ones, too much given, too great a tear. His contact functioning, more realistic, more hallucinated, partly depended on life's vicissitudes (Eigen, 1986: Chs 2, 7).

It often seems that hallucinations and delusions try to bind, express, sooth a sense of injury. In discussing Freud, I once wrote (1986: 47) "Wounded wishes find a home in hallucinations". And, (1986: 41) "The dream is a kind of pearl created around an irritant, dissolving pain by representing it." Dreams try to work with traumatic impacts *and* get rid of them, sometimes toning them down so that they *can* be worked with. One tries to make contact with self and other and play contact down enough so that contact can be sustained. Hallucination may play a role in making contact, e.g., in feeding and intensifying intuition. Connections between hallucination and reality may be more pervasive than believed. Hallucinated reality or aspects of reality may be more widespread than we like to think. It is unclear to what degree what we call reality is free of hallucination and delusion.

The notion that hallucination and delusion play an important role in our relation to reality gains impetus if, as Bion thinks, dreaming is part of waking as well as sleeping. Dreaming informs mental activity. Pain we try to get rid of finds its way into dreaming. Emotional irritants never totally dissolve. They re-form and press us through our dreams, as well as through inchoate pressures that tease representational ability. Core agonies, often eluding ability to name them, haunt the margins of our lives.

What does all this have to do with Kathryn? I go off on tangents. Sometimes in sessions I feel like a deep-sea diver with an urge to go deeper, find stranger, more fascinating fish. When I surface things are strange too. My contact function alters so that no place is a stranger to strangeness. I have wondered about contact since my teens. Why the need to make contact with strangers from outer space? It's hard enough making contact with neighbors. From an early age I knew how dangerous it was for one culture to make contact with another. One didn't have to be in a concentration camp to be changed forever by movies of them.

I can't help seeing concentration camp aspects of self wherever I look. This is probably unfair to patients. To look at Kathryn and see a concentration camp survivor, a victim, what good can this do? My God, she's right to be edgy. Therapy creates traumas of its own.

Look at her analysis, the one she most values, closest to a dream analysis, which supported her essence. As in so many dreams, a traumatic core surfaces. Her analysis supports her growth as a person, her personal being, and leaves her with wounds. A broken analysis she got so much from. Getting more than she hoped made her hope for more. Wounds from a broken analysis touching broken parts of self. Now she gathers those wounds and looks for someone to help dream them.

To have a successful dream is not just to feel better, to succeed in wish-fulfillment, but to nibble on what is bothering one a little more. Nibbling on what is bothering one sooner or later brings one to a nameless irritant built into life, an agony that remains invisible no matter how one names it. Exploding dream bubbles challenge us to become artists of the invisible.

If *contact* is a bad word, then contact means or is linked with trauma. Something bad happens if there is contact and something bad if there is no contact. Kathryn feels contacted by her therapist: connection made, support, recognition, realization of personal being. Kathryn's therapist opened herself to contact. Openness resonates. It touches Kathryn's desire to open, providing tastes of openness. Kathryn begins to open, wants more, risks more. Her therapist leaves. Kathryn must face the quandary, to open or close. She's face to face with raw material of self, wounded opening.

She left an earlier wounding therapy that starved her and found a nourishing one that wounded her. There are better and worse ways to be wounded and to approach wounding processes. There is no one way to be with the wound at the center of being. Giving is good but one never knows when or how the wound will overtake one. How can a therapy that gives so much be so wounding? How can it not?

I believe that a decent session gives rise to pulling back, re-grouping, thrusting, testing. Pointy, quivery quills. With some people you see armor, weapons. You have time to duck, fend off, come from another place. Kathryn's defense is made of millions of tiny bones quivering like crazy. She tries to tauten skin but you see little bubbles of jelly. Seeing is almost tactile, in some way *is* tactile. Psychic pointillism. Sticky burs in your eyes, not very stinging, like tiny bones in fish you have to chew very carefully. I pull at the burs heaped inside me. They accumulate over time. No one knows how, we seep into each other. My hands get buried in fuzz. An imperative drifts between my bones: "Don't rush!"

Thought drifts to watching "Three, Two, One – Contact" with my children. It was not a show I watched often. Something about science? Electricity? Magnetism? The cosmos awash with mysterious modes of contact? There is an undercurrent of mysterious forces between people. We used to speak of chemistry, electricity, attraction-repulsion in grade school, as teens. To have a crush on someone. Crushes – awesome word.

Use of "contact" in psychoanalysis. Bion's (1962: 17) contact barrier, an imaginary function to express permeability, flow, blockage between unconscious-conscious processes. Contact between functions and structures, old brain, new brain, right-left hemispheres, memory-perception, id-ego-superego.

Freud plays both ends against the middle. He depicts a primary out of contact dimension and an emerging contact function, the latter partly growing from impingement of stimuli on the cerebral cortex. We are in and out of contact at the same time. Freud goes so far as to see our sense of external space as a projection of inner space. Bion gives this theme a turn, linking our sense of outer space with a sense of affective fullness-emptiness (not just milk, feeling). Being filled or empty with emotion makes our sense of outer space possible. Originary space is affective space.

It would take a long time to begin to explore what in and out may mean. Similarly, it is too much for this chapter to explore what one is contacting when one is out of contact. The fact that we somehow recognize our struggle to make or break contact is widely expressed in sports, where contact or its lack wins or loses games (e.g., bat with ball, avoiding a tag). The fact that our sense of contact varies with conditions and moods makes us question and wonder about ourselves, adds to a sense of different worlds of experience, more or less boundless. Bion (1992: 372; Eigen, 1986, 1998) calls primary emotional reality *infinity*.

I think of the first moments of my first child's out of womb existence, his gaze into an infinite horizon. What does he see, where is he looking? Babies gaze at Eternity and we see God when we look into a baby's eyes. Infinitely precious being in the flesh.

Kathryn's life and therapy keep breaking infinity, premature infinity breakage. She acts as if contact is not problematic. She feels she knows what contact is but has problems doing it. She is afraid to open, but when she *can* open she values the experience and feels more valuable. She *knows* what she must do, yet fears it. She seems to have a clearer view of reality than I do, although she feels emotionally blocked. Self is more problematic for me, mysterious. My uncertainty as to what constitutes identity frightens her. She fears a sense of mystery. She knows who she is and who she wants to be, if only she could embody it.

When she bristles, I wonder who is bristling and fill in blanks, cover ignorance, say in a common sense way, "Kathryn is bristling." "Kathryn is protecting herself." "She is drawing back, afraid to go too far, fearful to stick herself out and get too hurt." "She is angry at me."

Why wonder who is bristling or what bristling is? Who is it who wonders? "Can't you take things at face value?" my mother used to say, a dumfounding remark. Faces are extraordinary.

When Kathryn enters the room, she enters the field of my challenged contact function. I sympathize with her skittishness about working with me. If I were working with me, I'd be skittish too. I am hyper-aware of how changeable my sense of contact is. A patient can never be sure what awaits them. This is true of any contact between any people anywhere. But in therapy there is special focus on making contact, a chance to become aware of *contact fantasies*, fantasies about therapeutic contact. Two people in the room focusing on how they make contact with each other.

An act of contact melds diverse, often conflicting tendencies. The locution, "an act of . . ." is misleading, since we are speaking of something more nebulous, evasive, involving plural processes and possibilities. Contact involves swirls of emotional pressures, often vague, sometimes insistent. We touch each other and ourselves through many atmospheric crosscurrents, always more going on than we can keep track of or digest.

Psychoanalysis often says that increased capacity for contact involves increased ability to undergo suffering. A person works towards sustaining intense psychic pressures. For example, Winnicott (1988: 80) writes, "Probably the greatest suffering in the human world is the suffering of the normal or healthy or mature person." Suffering is part of health. The more psyche, the more suffering. One makes oneself smaller to avoid pain.

A corollary to the idea that one curtails development in order to avoid suffering is: the more one cares, the more open to suffering one becomes. One truncates caring to downplay pain. Contraction of psychic contact is not simply a matter of conscious will or intention. Pulling back, shrinking, tightening, a kind of chronic inside wince or spasm, becomes set in ways that are hard to influence.

Winnicott advocates building receptivity to extremes of experience. He has in mind, in part, sheer appreciation of life's emotional color. In my experience, there are ways to go through agony that perforate the psyche and open new psychic pathways. One never knows when this will happen, but at the point I am writing, Kathryn and I seem far from it.

We are in a smaller phase. I feel tightness in myself that I feel in Kathryn, tightening around the bristles, tightening to avoid the bristles. To get close to oneself means getting stuck or cut by sharp things or sometimes falling into amorphous fudge between bristling. Pulling back and squeezing is habitual. Often we draw back to take a break from life, recovery time, but the spasm I am describing is linked with fearful helplessness.

I see something in her eyes and cheeks and chin that is hard for me to get to. Perhaps I'm afraid to find what it is I'm sensing. Her chest caves in a little. I see a person – where does this come from? what gives me the right to say it? – in danger of being torn apart. She scuttles to a safe retreat, trying to stay on top. Bristling and shrinking are part of the same movement, pulling back to a smaller self, an area one imagines one can control or hide in. Perhaps the fuller self Winnicott describes is not for everyone, perhaps moving in that direction is just too unbearable. When I'm with Kathryn I think, "Who *can* do it? Why *must* we try?" The cruelty of trying. Doesn't Kathryn's search for therapy express a wish to try? A wish she is stuck circling around?

One hint that there is more is the way she speaks of her husband. She feels she has the larger existence and is the bigger person. She has a better job, does more, makes more money, takes care of the kids more or sees to it that they are taken care of. He does what he can. She loves him. They care for each other. She appreciates him. *But.*

She runs their social life. He wants more time to himself. He likes solitary work, reading, writing, drawing. She needs to be with people to feel herself. He needs to be alone to feel himself. She puts him down for resisting social dates she arranges. He'll go along, enjoy them to a point, but she wants him to enjoy them more. She is more critical of him than he of her. It's OK with him for her to socialize, but it's not OK with her for him to be by himself.

She can not be by herself without feeling anxious. For her, social anxiety is more calming that alone anxiety. As often happens in a marriage, partners choose each other to make up for missing functions in themselves. Each can do or be something the other can't. Kathryn's husband seems at ease with this division of labor, but the greater load rests on her.

She tells me he is happy alone for hours, tracing themes in literature, philosophy, art, following lines of associations wherever they take him, personal, cultural, current events. He sometimes publishes but nothing comes of it except what goes into the writing itself. He ecstatically traces signifiers of pain throughout the world, a poignant and beautiful way to spend time. She is right to be angry at him. She calls him names, obsessive, schizoid. She envies him, looks down at him. He is sicker than she, more in touch than she.

He is selfish and she is giving, except that she knows she does what she has to and he does what he must. They are being themselves, tyrannized by themselves. Neither could do what the other does. It sounds like she envies him more than he envies her. He likes the kind of contact he has with himself, with writers throughout history, with creativity. He thinks the contact she has with others is superficial. "We are vain in different ways," he tells her.

She bristles with tears. How can tears bristle? "It's been a long time," she says. "I dry cry. Never tears. I cry with you, relief that hurts." Her face looks so clean and thin. There is no soap that can get this shine. I appreciate her tears but the shine almost wipes them away. Where does this shine come from, I wonder. "A controlling naiveté," comes the answer, words in my mind. I am speaking with myself, my brain, my mind, whatever, a conversation in my head or wherever. I think it's my head at the moment. I can easily see how people hear voices.

A bewildered girl in the woods (where did that come from? that's what I see). Her therapist leaves, her husband is not social enough, not successful enough, not good enough this or that way. There is a semi-unconscious command structure or expectation: my therapist should not leave, my husband should be different. In a perfect or better world, things would be perfect or better.

She wants to be better. She wants to have more access to feelings, to be more in contact. But if she were more in contact she might not bear it. She would break apart. Her rage would be too much. She envies her husband for whittling life down to something comfortable for him. A life that would suffocate her. There is a tension in her life she can not bear, a tension that gets expressed through conflict with him.

She *knows* what life *should* be like and this *isn't it.*

Guilt. I'm doing Kathryn an injustice. I'm doing to her what she does to her husband. I'm doubting her style of existence.

I am mediating an imperative that shafts her: a sense that life should be otherwise, a critique of suffering, a sense that life should be easier. A hidden belief: *it should be easier to be a person.*

An imperative, a wish, a belief, that is in a way the opposite of Winnicott's announcement that caring opens suffering, the suffering stimulation of complexity as well as appreciation of trauma, impossibility, disability. A suffering in face of the rage at life for failing her. The suffering of what is, creativeness in face of what is. A suffering creativeness in the depths of what is.

It can't be that simple. I see her eyes peeking out of the bristles. She is taking aim.

She is hiding. She is showing herself a tiny bit. I have to wait her out. I want to see it through. She sees things about me that scare her, make her want to run. She fears I am like her husband (I have that side). When she looks at me she sees things she doesn't even know she sees, monster things, deformed underpinnings, meshes of chewed flesh. My psyche is not clean like her face. Now I know I was seeing the clean face of her psyche. She has not yet penetrated this cleanliness.

She has a face that engenders no shudders when others see her. An attractive face, a traumaless face. I feel her looking at me and sense I have a face she might not be able to take, might not want to take. I think I scare her because trauma shows, suffering shows.

An attractive face guards her psyche, squeezes juice out of her psyche. She makes her psyche small enough to fit her face. We are face to face in a threatening therapy world, the two of us.

CHAPTER THREE

Words

"When I speak I am conscious of my words taking aim. I'm aiming at an enemy. I can't tell you how much this hurts me. When I was a child I stuttered and I knew why. I knew my words were pellets to sink into others and explode or poison. Once inside the other, they knew what to do. A wounding intent was buried in their essence."

This is the third time Harry said this to me in the past two weeks. I do not feel his words exploding, poisoning. Perhaps I will. Maybe they will sneak up on me and go off without warning when I step on one, a mine going off when a thought or feeling brushes it.

Harry is affable. I am attentive. I believe mines are there. I believe he is tortured by a hostile mind. I understand what he says but do not feel it. We have been together half a year and are still getting the feel of what it is like to be together.

I ask, "Do other words carry other feelings?" I am thinking of words of joy or beauty.

"I'm not talking about *that*," Harry says. "*That* is not what I'm trying to get across to you. I *must* make you know that I'm a *killer*. Words *kill*. I must tell you this because I must kill you.

"I know this is talk therapy. We put feelings into words. But that is an odd locution. We put feelings into words like gas in a car? Like cream in a cake? We put murder into words but don't actually kill each other? But I must be sure you know that we *do* kill each other. Speaking is murderous. Words kill. Words kill in worse ways than knives. I kill, therefore I am. I kill, therefore I'm not. It's obvious but people don't see it. If they see it, they gloss over it and pretend it's not happening. They go on as if they are not killing each other. But murder is the medium of words and, deep inside, murder makes life real. Pain is a kind of compass. I locate myself via pain. I am where pain is. When I kill you, I am where you are. It is a hidden form of travel, from pain to pain, psyche to psyche. You can locate yourself in anyone anywhere via pain travel. Murder is a kind of universal vehicle.

"There is a devil in words. Evil slips into words, drives words. A devil of persuasive force frames the way words work on belief. There are words that lead to physical murder, words that maim, deform, stifle. Murder is proof of existence. If we can be murdered that means we are here. If we *were* murdered, we *were* here."

Harry's words shoot through me but do not lodge. I see and feel what he is saying but do not find *him*. He communicates an agony of truth, a truth I know. His face hides torment. He tries to show what is gnarled and narrow as words. But they do not pass through his face. They do not gather up a lot of body. The words come from truth but hit the air and dissolve. I reach for their impact but am left straining. His words carry a most intense communication, murder itself, but I am left wondering, where did their feeling go? I hear intensity, taste it, wait for it.

Harry pulls the string on his speech. He puts himself into his words, puts everything into them, then stops in mid-air, undoes them, reverses them so that they boomerang, so that he becomes their target. His words do not lodge in me or even get to me because they reverse flight in mid-air and return to him. He learned how to protect others from his killer words, but that did not stop him from needing to communicate their intent. It's as if he's driven to keep saying, "I'm a murderer, I'm a murderer, I'm a murderer," even if he mostly murders himself.

"There is something about language that is hostile," Harry says.

"Does it hurt to speak?" I ask.

"Yes and it hurts not to."

"A double hurt."

"A hurt with many sources. A hurting that goes on beneath words. It's more than the impossibility of saying anything, or of there being too much to say, or of not knowing what to say. A hurting that words can't stop. Sometimes words fuel the hurting. Words are worse than worthless. They fuel injury. They grow out of injury. They are born in the hurt we are. We try to express it, share it. We look at another face and acknowledge we are all part of it. I open my mouth to share this sense and something awful happens."

"Too big a break between sensing and speaking?"

"Break is a good word. Breaking, breakdown."

Incapacity in face of words. Incapacity in face of feeling. Incapacity in transitioning. W. R. Bion (1992: 173) writes: "The success of psychoanalysis lies so far not so much in bringing communication nearer, as in showing unmistakably the feebleness of our methods of communication even in the communication of disagreement." It hurts to communicate because of feeble ability. To not communicate hurts too, like the build-up of milk in a mother's breast.

Overwhelming immensity of the wordless. Words are like ants biting and chewing bits off immensity. Beginningless immensity that words never catch up with, that words help to create. Immensity on the one hand, hole on the other. The famous hole in words, a hole in immensity. An immense hole in the human. Superabundance, deficit, impoverishment. Hyper-plus, zero, hyper-minus. Emotional flooding and emptying, rise and fall of feeling, We dream of being overcome by ocean waves because we can drown, because another person can overwhelm us, because we breathe feeling as well as air.

"There is always failure of contact, but that isn't murder," Harry says.

We are at a loss.

Harry rarely seems at a loss for words but words do not satisfy him. He recites parts of the psychoanalytic catechism. Portions of psychoanalysis are obnoxiously repetitive, emphasis on noxious. There must be a connection between feelings and words if the method of free expression works, if feelings undergo transformation through a kind of speaking. We look closely to see how this works and float out to sea.

It's not just feelings changing, how we feel in life, about life, how it feels to be alive. It is also our approach to feelings, our relationship to feelings, the attitudinal context and feel of feelings.

Voice One: Words do not mediate cure when they are murderous.

Voice Two: Isn't killing part of cure?

Voice One: Hurting makes saying worthless.

Voice Two: Hurting makes saying precious.

I am baffled. Let us say hurting goes on beneath words and words partly are born out of hurt to express the wordless, to take hurting to another level, to supply being with further stitches and complex tapestry. Harry focuses on hurting because he tries to find what hurts him, or tries to find how to work with hurt or live with it or diminish it, or perhaps even turn the hurt into an opening of self. We could say the same about words and wordless joy and chart how they add to and subtract from each other. People try to escape pain, but they try to escape joy as well. Harry, however, focuses on hurt.

"It is soul murder and more than soul murder," Harry gropes. "It includes my agony as a person, my trauma history. But part of it is murderous intent towards pain itself. Not simply words killing soul. Words express soul, give birth to soul. Words are soul colors – look at poetry. But in the hands of the wrong kind of murderer, they null soul, deform feeling, twist the body, warp everything. There is soul agony that murder does not stop. Soul agony murder tries to stop but becomes part of, adds to, perpetuates. It is a property of murder that it exacerbates the pain it tries to end."

Voice One: Wishful thinking! Many are the murders I feel good about. I free myself by killing pain.

Voice Two: You cauterize yourself, cut nerve endings, soul nerves.

Voice One: You like to think one pays for killing pain, for killing soul, killing self. The truth is, that is precisely what enables one to live, to make a go of it, to win, to taste glory.

There is religious death: to die to be reborn. There is political death: To die, to cut off pain, guilt, shame, to win. Political birth is always monstrous, necessary. There is no shortage of monstrous births. Happy, caring, inspiring looking monsters often make people feel good while they die. When religious and political monsters unite, watch out for shock and awe and horror, protected by an impenetrable lie shield. The impenetrable lie shield cloaks, if not blots out pain, but festers out of sight.

"The murder I am trying to find is not so easy to locate. It slides.

When you think you have it, it's somewhere else. A gliding murder, like a slug evacuating a trail wherever it crawls, except this evacuation is a murderous path killing whatever it touches. Words, sliding through the psyche, help create trail systems."

Voice Two: Words go beyond the trails they create and tilt the psyche towards the future.

Voice One: Always the optimist. Words as cocoons, rather than lethal paths. Our voices are interchangeable.

"I think the murder I am looking for has something to do with helplessness, fragility," murmurs Harry. "A futility in face of words *and* the wordless."

"A very deep murder," I say. "A place where it's hard to feel impact, your own or others."

"Or where impact doesn't matter," he adds. "Where impact doesn't impact."

I tell Harry two stories about lack of impact. A woman in an encounter group in the 1960s said she didn't hear her voice. It was soundless. It didn't affect others. It couldn't elicit response. It had no impact. The group leader asked her to scream and she screamed loud and long with all her might. We heard her very well. She had a lot of nuances in her scream: fury, fear, pleading, wishing, longing, exasperation, futility, hopelessness, need, demand, hurting, loneliness, helpless power. So many emotions in a scream, like a prism refracting colors. Her scream triggered feeling in others. Still, she did not feel it. She could not hear her scream. It sounded softer than a whisper. For her, her voice did not fill space, as if space were too immense, a void so great that emotion died out in it.[1] She could not feel her echo in the other, it did not come back to her. There was a deficit of the kind of human space where feelings count. Perhaps this is a bit of what Harry means by murder: deprivation of a place where feelings grow. Not simply that feelings hurt, but the place that fails to grow feelings hurts, an uninhabitable place we can't get rid of.

An obverse example of no impact involved a moment on the football field when my body disappeared. It was an informal game in Central Park in my twenties. I was guarding the passer and a man I was supposed to block rushed towards me. He was bigger and stronger and I expected him to run over me. At best, I could slow him down. Now, more than forty-five years later, I have not digested the fact that he and other tacklers in that play bounced off of me. They were weightless and had no impact at all. I watched with astonishment. Instead of my being slammed to the ground, *they* were on the ground. It's almost as if I had no role in it. I remember thinking, O my God, here they come. I had to make a split second decision whether to fake blocking them or to give it all I had even if futile. I chose the latter or, rather, the latter happened. Yet I felt like silly putty or a hole in a Henry Moore sculpture, as if I offered no resistance. I felt neither them nor me. We were all weightless, light. I understood I impacted, without feeling how.

Harry wonders if he and I are weightless and will bounce off each other or whether we will have ill impacts. He envies me my good experience, with echoes of a sense of wonder of his own. He is more amazed than irritated that I don't feel the murderous impact of his words and being. He knows I believe in psychic killers. Why can't I feel *his*? Why can't I feel the killer *him*? If I can't feel the killer, can I feel *him* at all?

I tell Harry another anecdote about a woman in a body group who could not feel her impact. The leader had her bang a pillow. She beat it with all her might until exhausted. We took turns holding the pillow and some of us nearly fell backwards from the force of her blows. But like the woman who screamed in what felt to her a soundproof room, this woman's blows landed in a vacuum. Soundless voice, forceless blows. Life without impact.

How this happens, we are not sure. But we know it happens. For Harry, these anecdotes are a bit like Zen stories, his life a kind of Zen story. How can killer words not impact? These stories don't exactly make him feel less alone. But something is heard, something is shared, even if impact is not felt or felt strongly enough. At least he knows the unreal no-impact state that he links with helpless, futile fragility is real.

He glares at me, draws back, gathers himself. His eyes redden. "Easy for you to talk. Maybe you can kill and feel it. It's worse when you kill and can't feel it. I *know* I put words inside people that hurt them. But the pain I cause goes on without me. It glances off me like the tacklers bounced off you. I am not brought down by the pain I cause. It is weightless, groundless silly putty. No one feels it. I cause pain that no one feels, psychic murder without traces. No one catches me or puts me on trial or gets back at me in any way that counts.

"It's brutal to kill people without their knowing it and they go on as if they were alive. As if murder does not touch them. The opposite of the experience you recount. No one falls down to the ground. Everything goes on as it was. Don't they know they are being corroded, annihilated? Hate is hollowing their insides, creating malignancies, and they are oblivious, shrug it off. They give no sign they are aware of what I'm doing to them."

His depiction of murdering people without their knowing it, their going on as if nothing happened, is chilling. I know he is right, this happens. I suspect it happens often. People hollowed out by word murder they are unaware of.

I realize I tried to stuff him with my stories about impact-less states and that his outrage brought out a clearer, more intense statement of his truth. I draw back, nibble at edges, ready to plunge in a little more. I believe in the hurt and hate but there is still a way I do not feel it. I have an inkling that *not feeling murdered* is a clue to the futile helplessness and fragility Harry said was basic.

Something is happening but I can not contact it. Perhaps I do not have to contact it. It may enter awareness at some point and I can greet it and we can get acquainted. But it goes on anyway.

So much intensity and vacancy. Murdered beings with no insides, looking alive, as if stuffed models of animals and people in a natural history museum populated Harry's life. I get a glimpse of him as an infant surrounded by people he hollowed out. Every infant is an explorer discovering murders built into life, not knowing what to do with such discoveries. They are left with whole areas of non-communication of the most important facts.

There are many kinds of murder and areas that get murdered or partly murdered. So many feelings get damaged and grow misshapen. Monsters are very important to the human psyche. They express strangulated states that feelings undergo. Words are like buckets drawn from wells of feeling, buckets with random patterns of holes. You never know what you will find or lose. Sometimes eyes appear in a bucket, eyes staring into the fragile immensity we feel when we breathe. It is important for a baby to stare into the immensity of breathing and relax into vast darkness surrounding light. But if darkness and light are too frightening, there is no place to stare. Eyes begin staring at themselves, at their inability; monster eyes glued to their own strangulated state.

Do monster eyes see only monsters? Sometimes we portray monsters in love with beauty, tormented by beauty, sometimes killing beauty. Does something else get through? Is there sound if not heard, impact if not felt? Harry believes so but belief baffles him. He wants corroboration but it is difficult receiving corroboration if it is not felt. Therapy works in fields of mutual impact, even if impact is elusive, even if it is not felt. If necessary, therapy gravitates towards places of no-impact, no-feeling. Not being as a mode of being and being as a mode of not being. There are instances in which therapy seeks the uninhabitable and lives there until no-impact, no-feeling penetrates and is more fully acknowledged. Our faith in therapy goes on with or without us, whether or not we feel real, whatever mixture of feeling there and not there. Our hope is that we will be included in its movement with benefit.

* * *

A baby is crying. An angry, fearful baby. Anger is scarcely the word to describe strangulated furies triggered by an infant's fathomless distress. Distress infinitizes into bottomless agonies. Emotion, body, self heave together, overlapping waves. Mother is apprehensive, caring, quiets the infant, soft talks the baby out of tears and fears. The infant grows calm, the storm passes, a change of emotional somatic weather, a change of spirit, the return of goodness. Rise and fall of storms happen repeatedly. Goodness comes through. A basic rhythm of coming through difficulty develops, trust in good outcomes.

What went wrong with Harry? When mother came, he could not let anger dissolve? The anger held him, he held it to the bitter end? Goodness was not good enough to dissolve it? He could not let himself pass out in bliss in mother's arms? He refused to be fobbed off by goodness or what offered itself as good? Was he hyperconscious of a negative side to goodness? To dissolve anger was to suffocate or dissolve the self? Does something in a baby need to subvert as well as enjoy goodness? Was Harry born with unusual awareness of what is lost in soothing? Was there something in mother's face that stopped him, shocked him, a Medusa aspect we (and babies) try to ignore, displace, project, mythologize? Babies tighten and relax in mother's arms, fight and surrender. Did the tight-fight aspect in Harry's case take on too great intensity? Why couldn't Harry ignore it and go under and go on like the rest of us?

In Harry's case, consciousness mutated, maintained awareness of anger dissolving. No baby can simply hold on to anger forever but I wonder if some babies have greater awareness while in the process, a kind of hyperawareness of aspects of what they go through. This is a possibility I postulate (not dogmatically) with Harry. Rage begins to dissolve in bliss, as mother makes things nice. Nevertheless, he never completely lets go, remains partly tight, holding fast, gripping. Yet partly dissolves, goes under, gives in to the swoon, the comfort, while remaining aware of what is happening, something like staying awake while one sleeps or remaining on heightened alert while passing out. One sees what is happening as one goes under.

In Harry's case, he does not give up the anger as mother makes nice, yet partly goes under, dissolves, moves on. He does not wholly give up his grip on what mother soothes, but remains attached to it, with this difference: he makes a radical discovery that, in some way, what is in him has no effect, *his* rage or fury has no impact. This realization heightens murderous intent, with no further impact or result. His insides fail to affect another in a way that he can feel. Of course, this is not entirely true. There are ways he affects the other and ways he doesn't. Somehow, in this drama, there is a way that a portion of fury slips by without result and that registers, magnifies, becomes a center of psychic significance.

The fact that his distress and fury attract mother's attention, call her to him, initiate concern and soothing behavior, is lost on him, doesn't seem to matter to an aspect of his rage. The link between scream and comforting response may have positive consequences for other aspects of Harry's personality. But for some portion of fury or rage or agony it is besides the point. *There is something that rage wants, something that murderous intent wants, that soothing does not satisfy.* And it is here that Harry is stuck. It is this kernel of dissatisfaction, lack of effect, lack of impact, that forms a nucleus of consequence for Harry's experience of life.

"I've come here to regain myself," Harry urged. "To regain what goodness killed."

"You can't stop killing . . ." I murmur. We tear at the tissue of thought until thought vaporizes. Tear at *ourselves* until *we* vaporize. Does this kind of murder begin in infancy? Baby killers fascinate popular imagination because there is truth in this fantasy. Baby as scientist, the questioning stare, inquisitive reaching, refusing to be bought off. Curiosity and the drive to know, pushing past comfort and goodness, pushing into them. An inquisitional spec of the human psyche, a need to get to the bottom of things, to get at truth. Baby's anger as seedbed and nest for the human race's murderous bent. It can and often does take wrong and disastrous turns.

"Killing that no one feels," Harry says. "I expect signs, look for hurt faces, expect blood to pour, ooze from places words hit. With all the killer words flying around I expect humanity to collapse in a heap and I would be alone. But, nothing. We invent bullets, weapons to make visible what words invisibly do. Weapons to show what we do emotionally but lack language for. Words are not enough."

To damage ourselves and others with weaponry gives some expression to inexpressible injury. We lack language strong enough to communicate the press of feelings. Physical damage can be seen and felt, emotional damage remains elusive. We can point to burnt bodies with horror or pleasure, giving some satisfaction to boundless emotions that remain out of reach. Harry has hit upon the discovery that the force of words insufficiently mediates the boundless intensity emotional reality seeks. Even words filled with murder fall short.

We have come a long way. A murderer who knows he murders in such a way that no one knows or feels it. "Everyone is a killer," reflects Harry. "Everyone is murdering everyone and no one knows it." Harry seemed satisfied he had reached something. "You can 't experience something that's always there," he adds. "But we do."

* * *

Harry's chest heaves. Contractions in chest and stomach. Dry tears. "If I move this way, I don't feel pain. I don't cry." He semi-doubles over, holds himself.

"Try breathing more intensely," I suggest.

He does but nothing happens.

"I sense agony in a void but don't really feel it," he says.

I wonder aloud if there is always a void in the agony or whether it is especially intensified because of an indiscernible void in parental responsiveness. A void in parental emotionality.

There is void as defense against feeling and void in feeling itself.

"I'm losing it. My mind's drifting. I think of emotional junk food. People over-dosing on emotionality, making themselves sick. That's void in emotionality, emotionality as void. But it takes me away from myself."

He is quiet awhile, then speaks for a long time.

"When I dry cry my chest contracts and I don't feel the feeling. I know there are people who are really numb. That's not my problem. I'm not numb. I know about people filling deadness with murderous intensity. Some feel deadness with murderous intensity. I called you after reading *Psychic Deadness*. I was writing on deadness as a theme in poetry, then came across your book and saw we vary along a deadness-aliveness gradient. I hadn't been as conscious of that before. You can feel agony being a little alive or a lot alive.

"We try to keep ourselves in super-life to avoid the agony of living. Nowadays we are ashamed of falling out of hyper-life. We get pumped up with images of how we should be and how really successful people are doing. It's quite depressing. We try to maintain feeling up by medication, afraid to drop down and not come back. The need to keep functioning at a high level, the fear of not being able to show up and do what we have to do, keeps us afraid of the gradient. It is like fearing to fall off the edge of the emotional universe, as if it were flat. Medication provides a net.

"I've worked hard to get off meds. It's been an awful struggle. I don't know if I can stay off, but right now it's worth it."

We are quietly listening to our breathing, the noise outside: a child cries and a mother chastens it, a delivery man chains his bicycle to the bars on my window. Harry breaks into tears. How language captures the sense of breaking, breaking open, breaking down, breaking up, breaking free. "He finally broke down," I heard someone say about a man weeping at a funeral.

Harry weeps and weeps.

"The mother yelling at the child was too much. When I heard the bike chains I thought, 'She is chaining the child.' I have an urge to step outside and breathe, to unchain the child. I want to give that mother a softer voice. When I hear her voice I stop breathing. My soul stops breathing. My breath contracts around the pain. I'm breathing cautiously, breathing around the pain. Around bullet sounds, bullet words. My breath cushions the shots.

"Now my chest is starting to relax. Soul is in my chest, returning through my chest."

I too cringed at the mother's metallic, scraping tone. To scold, to make cold. I could feel my insides tightening, soul tightening all through my body. A tongue lashing is a kind of beating. The emotional and physical meld. When Harry and I thawed out some, my hand involuntarily went to my heart.

Harry does not have to draw blood to see soul. He knows words encode and create affect, are parts of emotional fields. Some people *do* have to draw blood in order to feel soul. Words are a kind of emotional blood. For writers, words are a life blood. There is soul in words.

Thus, too, words can be soul killers. The mother's sharp tongue mediated death. Rage without words would not be as sharp, unless actual weapons were used to penetrate the body, Rage mediated through words intimidates, chills, tries to strip the other of power. To castigate, to reduce to obedience, to freeze. Harry and I felt the child outside stop breathing.

Injustice antedates words. I suspect a sense of injustice embeds in the psyche in early infancy. The parent's greater physical strength overpowers the child. Parental emotional whimsy and physical power career through a child's being. Sometimes there is great care, great attunement. But parental caprice often over-rules an infant's will and reality. A backlog of wordless, boundless injustice readies to spill into words and social forms. By the time we speak, there are aeons of wordless grievances that can never be redressed.

Part of the background of wordless grievance turns into Satan. Satan expresses a background of sensed injustice that weaves with bounty. The stream of felt injustice is incompletely channeled by persecuting, accusatory words: justice as an agent of persecution. In the Bible, Satan is an accuser, a strict reader of the law. Flaws and trespasses are magnified by Satan's keen eye and trickster tongue. To use law to ensnare, to trick souls into massive self-hate, self-doubt; to use truth to stymie, to blame rather than disclose.

"When I was hospitalized, my head was swimming in words, everything creepy with meaning. Words piled on words, meaning on meaning. A dread, a malignancy tinged them all. *That* was Satan. A thing about Satan was: he rejoiced in my fear. A twisted, paralyzing joy. My anger was ineffectual. Fear was the main thing. Everything turned into fear. Fear made me strong, made me food for Satan. It was the scariest thing to see my fear make Satan's eyes gleam. Could it be I saw my mother's smile as satanic? My gentle, caring mother soothing me with a Satanic gleam that jolted me out of my skin?

"I don't believe it. I've gotten to a place where I distort everything. Everything *is* distorted. Distorting mirrors express this a tiny bit. Twisted bodies and faces express the way feelings get twisted out of shape. The title of your book: *Reshaping the Self*. Did you know about melting faces, disfigured feelings? Longing solicited Satan but fear drove him.

"Clean words are worse than bloody words. Words that sanitize the bloody mess inside. The father of lies leaves no lie unturned. Satan wants a lie cleaned world, the biggest lie of all. Dirty words are better."

Satan as lie finder. Sanitized sanity as screen for the worst warps. What about Satan as curiosity, as life drive? Curiosity kills cats but it's worse to be brain dead. How did Satan get to be so negative? Aren't there worse things than negative? Did Satan go overboard and ruin a good thing? When does inquire become inquisition? Does a satanic thread thrive on a basic connection between nourishment and murder, to eat, to hate? Isn't it important to be critical?

"Words eat words," said Harry. "They dissolve each other, extract nutrients. Words have digestive tracts in which acids work on mute thunder. Experience turns itself over inside words. I watch people in the park on wheels. Roller blades, wheelies, skate boards, bikes, scooters, all kinds of gliding, like meanings flying just above the ground defying gravity. When talk comes successfully we say we're on a roll.

"You're a wordsmith. You use words to reconfigure twisted feelings. You touch twisted affect with the magic wand of words. When I say I am communicating I am voiding feeling. When I walked out the hospital door I felt filled with the cipher of myself. Something anger can't get to. I am nothing. It is comforting to say that.

"Sometimes you seem to like being with me. At this moment I like being with you a lot.

"A seizure is happening, a plunge. I see a most awful thing. A strangulated baby, a baby that can't breathe. Maybe it's stuffed with too much emotion or a vacuum. Too much is a void. Am I feeling sorry for myself? The worst thing is the baby's mangled body. A baby tightens, strangles itself with its muscles all through its body because it is afraid to breathe in the emotional air.

"My mother is kind. I am afraid to breathe her goodness. It will suffocate me. The baby sees a mother's helplessness, her anguish. Something is wrong. The mother's milk stops. There is not enough. The baby is starving and thinks it is suffocating. Or is it the reverse? The baby is turning blue. When the baby is older the blue will be in the back and it will be called depression. A gripping from deep inside. There's nothing wrong with mother's feelings, a sweet mother, a caring mother. Caught between deaths, trapped in a continuum.

"The baby lets the mother fall. The mother drops the baby. A breath of air. To injure makes us feel free.

"Little by little, artists among us notice a horror: attempts to free ourselves create poisonous bonds.

"The baby is mother's joy, yes? And the mother's helpless fear."

No air, no nourishment = too much air, too much nourishment. Injury makes us real. Injury scares us into unreality.

"She does not know what to do with me. I am her fear. Anger unites us, makes us go away. Fear unites us, drives us apart. I don't see any way out. I am her helplessness, her strangulated baby life. I try to scream her fear away but it reforms. To scream fear away is to scream myself away. I have to stop eating, stop breathing. Maybe things were better before I was born. Before I was a day old."

Harry found that a negative vision helped organize a fairly successful life. He had a kind of charisma. People liked to hear him. With me, he revealed a herniated psyche trying to fly. I liked listening to him too, a painful kind of pleasure. I felt like I was sliding on a narcissistic coating around a secret wound, into embalmed helplessness stuffed with maternal fear. His words dipped deeply into wordlessness.

To speak inside the wordless, words steeped in wordlessness. To see images that can't be seen, imageless images of an ache aching, a painful background ache, like the background radiation of the universe, a background trauma ache without graspable beginning or end.

Is the background radiation of the psychic universe joy or trauma? Beauty everywhere. The music of the spheres is not only in the stars but in our bodies, our sensations, feelings, thoughts. We are, after all, music making beings. We *have to* make music to express something essential about existence, the way life feels. Our job is to uphold the beautiful, not to denigrate it, while not losing the unbearable. Our job is to listen to what's there.

I stay at unbearable points only a short time before loss of awareness. I can't bear the unbearable very well. A quiet immensity enters when I think about things and I feel incapacity. Harry is often in the room without me. I simply can not go everywhere he must. A wordless immensity in the corner like a cat comes closer, curls under the couch. I fear it will stiffen because of pain in the air. But it not only stiffens. It is curvy, sinuous. My fear that it will suffocate fades. I am breathing again. The cat liquefies my body. I can not hold on to anything. There are no straight lines in water.

"I feel we are getting somewhere," Harry tells me.

"I feel so too," I say.

Note

1. Bion (1970: 12) says of surgical shock, "the dilatation of the capillaries throughout the body so increases the space in which blood can circulate that the patient may bleed to death in his own tissues. Mental space is so vast compared with any realization of three-dimensional space that the patient's capacity for emotion is felt to be lost because emotion itself is felt to drain away and be lost in immensity."

CHAPTER FOUR

Trauma Clots

Arnie lived a full life at the edge of depression. He was born in the south, warm weather, warm water. He feels that the women who cared for him, along with his mother, over-fulfilled him. They gave him too much of everything: beach, swimming, boating, fishing, endless play, lots of attention, paradise. This, he claims, is the first bane of his life, things came too easy. He was not prepared for what lay ahead. He wonders, too, about sexual molestation, vague images, sensations, a woman mouthing his penis, a man doing something, wanting to do something, sensations in the background of his feeling self.

When he was ten his father took the family to live in a "bad" neighborhood in a northern city. Tough kids, fights, struggle for survival. Arnie didn't know what hit him, yet the challenge excited him, his first true test beyond mama's care. He suspected his easy life was illusory. Now he had a chance to taste the truth of pushing against one's limits, the limits of the world.

Arnie relished exercising his powers but there were flickers of sadness. He missed southern ease, the caring rhythms that once fed him. New pleasures, new injuries. Sadness stayed and there was no way of knowing the turns sadness would take over time.

In Arnie's teens, his father died and his mother became depressed. By the time he finished college, she was permanently hospitalized. When he visited her, she offered to service him until he got a wife. His father left him enough money to get through college. Arnie suffered breakdowns as a young man but finished school and worked hard. He had affairs, married, raised a family and made a living. He was successful enough to help a number of people along the way. At the same time, he spoke about acts for which he could not forgive himself; black marks that would not go away.

His children married and became parents, his grandchildren a source of extreme delight. I often thought they kept him alive. At our first meeting he announced he would kill himself within a year, a remark that never left me. I held my breath as the year passed, and another year, and another. I was grateful for his grandchildren. What is important is not only love, but capacity to feel it filled with enough meaning to keep life afloat. The light and pain of his grandchildren's lives gave Arnie that meaning.

Nothing pained him more than his grandchildren's pain. His own pain might be more severe, more menacing, but theirs was more real. *His* pain was part of a massive collapse, chronic, ongoing. Theirs was the round, three-dimensional pain of fully living souls.

Not that Arnie wasn't alive. His life was not merely a half life. The situation was more wrenching. It is hard to pin down the area of hell that smeared his insides. I think of Gaudi-like twists of metal, squeezing agony out of evil being, gnarled suffering. Gaudi's twisted metal brings soul sickness into focus. Hard metal as mysterious, marauding presences. What eats at Gaudi, eats at us. When I leave his buildings I am amazed I am intact, less flayed than compressed, certain that rats gnawed my flesh to the bone.

I feel something of this twisted compression in Arnie, although the twists are invisible, the menace impalpable. His face is pleasantly disarming. There is softness, a likeable breast quality. You think you can get close and, for moments, you *can*. It is, at first, hard to believe that there is mocking laughter in his head, that he is laughing at your ills, happy over your pain. It is difficult to believe that his sincerity is a mock-up, that his goodness harbors a scoffer, a cruelty he can not help. Still, I can not stop believing in his sweetness. A big mistake, he warns. I know, I know. Gaudi's metals express damnation, something Arnie feels keenly. His face collapses, his voice becomes forlorn.

His grandchildren touch him beneath his doubleness. Doubleness continues but does not have the only word. Life goes on as usual. He works, makes decisions, takes care of things, supports others. An active, caring man with a secret. After work he spends gobs of time in bed staring blindly. He insists he is a ghoul.

The mocker, a heh-heh devil, cackled ever since he can remember, but the ghoul needed time to grow. It provided the bodiless cackle with a place. The mocker was there since childhood but it wasn't until adulthood that Arnie turned into a ghoul. At first the ghoul was a transient cloud passing from time to time. Then it thickened into an atmosphere, part of the atmosphere of collapse, hiding sun for longer periods. The ghoul was slow to develop but, in the past decade, grew into an almost steady presence.

It takes a lot of patience to work with a ghoul. When you think you know it, it turns into something else. But certain characteristics were clear in a messy sort of way. A lot of darkness, amorphous blackness with variable clots and spreads. A lot of hate and self-hate sprinkled with self-pity. A sense of collapse or semi-collapse, offset by a malignant inner glare, a nasty turn of mind. Hopelessness. And somewhere in the hopelessness, obscure, bottomless pain.

In the outside world, the psychiatric diagnosis is depression, treated with medication. The inside world, though, is alive with crawling, slithering things, evil whispers, taunts and jeers, slimy brews, oozes of wrath percolating in moldy cauldrons, teeming dead seas, nearly invisible, inaudible squirmy, wormy squeals. A lot of death goes on in the deadness, many kinds of deaths within deaths.

Insides call to insides and pills may help but do not touch secret places where life grows with little or no light. What is left of soul is hollow, heavy, inert, dense, yet wriggling like a cut nerve. The man who houses this soul is semi-paralyzed in bed, spirit disappearing, gone, a cemented, sunken corpse twitching with severed life.

How is this different from the scoffer, the heh-heh devil? The scoffer is more organized, a wormy steel splinter inside Arnie's *head*, exploiting the man's eyes, superior atop the upright posture, surveying deprecatingly, seeing everything negatively. The soul maggots in the dark, heavy, wriggly, ooze, all the squirmy things packed in deadness, occupy the *body*, spread in flesh and organs, in the bloodstream, in respiration. They cover and infuse body and body spirit, congealing and vaporizing bone, nerve, flesh.

What is left of the body hovers over itself, quivering, waiting for prey, for alternate body souls to sink into, like one who becomes a vampire because of being vampirized. The ghoul is more amorphous than a vampire, gelatinous, darkly transparent, ready to change shape and consistency to pour through victims, becoming pools of fury and fear and nothing. The ghoul stings and clings, a filmy parasite. Arnie's ghoul's specialty is to threaten. It seems to prefer scaring the spirit out of people than actually bothering to occupy them. Even momentary frights satisfy it momentarily, although being frightening becomes addictive, consuming, a full time job.

The ghoul becomes fodder for the heh-heh devil.[1] In a brilliant tactical move, the heh-heh devil scoffs at the ghoul, pre-empting the latter's turf. It does this by accusing Arnie of being ghoulish, triggering circuits of self-accusation. Thus session after session Arnie comes in repeating, like a mantra, "I'm a ghoul." He is sheepish, confessional, dismal, disgraced, disgusted, compulsively luxuriating in shame and self-loathing. There is almost an exhibitionistic quality: Arnie needs to be sure the ghoul is seen and known, is somehow visible and tangible, although it can't be seen or heard. If he says it enough ("I'm a ghoul . . .") he can go on with the session. Not that he isn't ghoulish. It's just that the repetition provides enough release so that other things come out.

Arnie learned from his psychiatrist that he has a genetic loading for depression, a bad gene. Other family members, not only Arnie's mother, were psychotically depressed. The psychiatrist postulates an inherited chemical imbalance that medication helps to redress. I don't see how one can be sure of this conclusion, but it is fashionable today. I wouldn't be surprised to learn that the human race is chemically unbalanced. Wouldn't it be sounder for the psychiatrist to say, "Maybe this medication will help. We find it sometimes (often) does."

"I have a bad gene and am chemically unbalanced," becomes a mantra with organizing benefit at times. It also reinforces hopelessness. "Why try to struggle with oneself? You can't change your genes." This seems to tie things up too neatly. Who knows what life brings, how feelings and theories shift, another finding, vision, another experience? Already attitudes are broadening in ways that include both medication *and* therapy, since people hunger to speak about themselves, to contact themselves, to change, to open.

Arnie was lucky that medication worked up to a point but not completely. Arnie needed another person for support. He needed someone to know what it was like for him, to know the ghoul and scoffer, the morass, the evil. Talking sometimes was a kind of blood-letting, draining infection. But it was also an emotional exchange, a caring ear and voice, a sense of being with someone who knew what bad stuff was.

*   *   *

For many years, intermittently, Arnie felt close to a woman who made him smile. Her aliveness infused him. She meant life. Then something happened, something he did, and she clicked off. In a micro-moment, a bar shut. For months he dreamt of doors closing. They felt closed forever. He knew that for her, in an instant, the relationship died.

He knew. But *I* could not tell if he really knew or was translating a foreboding, a sense of doom, into something final. To experience a mood as absolute is characteristic of depression. Severed, injury without end, without reparation. This is not to say that something bad didn't happen. It also is possible Arnie is right, that his friend's feelings for him ended in a moment. Moments modify each other, for worse, for better. In this case, time stuck in a downswing. A victory for the ghoul, or heh-heh devil, or both.

Many moments in life are absolutized. Mystical states, falling in love, religious belief, devotion to a cause, ideology, leader.[2] A sense of *one*: there is only *one* college to go to, *one* person to be with, *one* way of being a psychoanalyst, *one* way to love God. Often it is *my* one at the expense of *yours*. One and possessiveness go together.

In psychosis, the sense that something is gone, altered, mutilated often goes with a sense of things having been better, a golden age before the break (fall). In Arnie's case, the happy time was life before his family moved north, before death and madness. Yet even in paradise, he vaguely felt life was somehow off, a sense he did not dwell on. Discontent in paradise seemed beatific in comparison with what came to pass.

In psychosis, the before-after structure transfers to many situations, in this case, to his friend's ruined feelings for him. *Before* they were golden, *then* everlasting shit, at least in his fancy. Realistic possibilities mean little when a doom template sucks reality and creates black winters. He failed to let in his friend's ticking, biological clock.

They shared times when they made each other happy but she wanted to have children, raise a family. He would never leave his wife. She didn't want to be alone forever. She wanted more. There were times when her aliveness saved him from depression. Its loss opened a hole.

Even sinking, he appreciated what she gave him. The gift of herself, an oasis, tastes of life's nourishment. Such things we live for. Nevertheless, aliveness is not easy. Arnie broke down in face of it, when he and his friend first drew close and again when they parted. He broke down when his first child was born and again after the birth of his first grandchild. Peak moments endangered him. Rise of life and its loss were too much. Arnie could not take doors opening *or* closing.

* * *

To dream of doors closing is to dream of death. But to close, a door must be open. We close or open more or less to help moderate our variable sense of aliveness-deadness (Eigen, 1996). Deadening helps to modulate life's impact. Several weeks after first dreaming of doors closing and the hopeless loss over his friend's change, Arnie spoke of a dead spot *and* a dread spot. For years, Arnie never budged from his belief that nothing was wrong with his mother when he was very young. She was normal before they moved, before his father's death, before her breakdowns. Another before-after.

One day the dead and dread spots came together. Arnie spoke of a dead spot in the dread spot and vice versa. A fantasy arose of a dead spot in his mother meeting a baby's dread. He was thinking of his mother and his wife. He did not think his wife was very good when their children were young. She screamed, turned off and on, raging and blank. "She was not a good mother," he told me many times. She got better as the children got older. The children paid a price, were scarred.

It was the opposite with him. When they were young, he gave them everything. His love was infinite. As they grew, his love became conditional, rigid, punishing. Children pay the price of parental personalities. His children got through, had jobs, families, in their own ways lived fully, but never fulfilled themselves vocationally. Their work life was stunted, enough to get by. Their marriages were difficult, unsatisfactory, but enduring. Arnie felt his children could have been more, done more, with more support. Yet they were not psychotic or seriously depressed and got on with things. They patched together enough to see them through. Arnie, at least, recognized that he did not pass on his sickness, but passed on a sense of deprivation, life lived at a lower flame.

He felt his children had at least one advantage over him: they knew where they stood from the beginning. They knew life was rough just by being exposed to parental extremes. He believed his early life to be more placid, even idyllic, and failed to prepare him for what came later. He had to learn on his own how rough things were without the luxury of childhood plasticity and resilience.

Awful surprise followed awful surprise, and while he met life's necessities, he suffered a semi-deflated spirit he came to call ghoulish. A ghoul plagued by a heh-heh devil, a body-ego ghoul and mentalized devil permeated by dread and deadness. He fears getting worse with age. His children got flattened out at an early age but learned to deal with it. He was falling, contracting, losing ground. His self-knowledge was of ongoing breakdown, a sense of shrinking. Even his degrading cynicism was shriveling.

I was surprised to hear him speak of a dead mother or part of mother inside his baby self. Always, he spoke as if his mother's depression came out of the blue, precipitated by moving, her husband's death, her children readying to leave home. He insisted that she was normal when he was young. Normal by contrast, perhaps. To be depressed is one thing, to need permanent hospitalization another. Now he envisions a deadness in mother exacerbating a baby's dread. His mother? Him as a baby? Whose dread? Whose deadness? Often deadness dampens anxiety. But a baby's anxiety, if met by deadness, spirals before it dulls.

Arnie's glimpse of dead/dread deflects into concern with violence. His wife's violence when the children were young, his own lapses that he feels horrible about after all these years. Soldiers dying, civilians dying, murder that goes on and on. News photos, TV, hints of horror. Suicide bombers a fact of daily life. "How many people will die, will kill themselves in this war?!" he exclaims. He feels suicidal. Mangled bodies, slaughter. "My slaughtered psyche can't take it!" he moans. I call his attention to the turn his speaking of deadness and dread took. After some time reflecting, he says plaintively, wryly, "Perturbations that enliven dread turn into slaughter."

Apprehension, his and mine, of spreading dreadful, self-deadening slaughter. War as anodyne, a deflection, providing place and reason for deadness and dread. A creator and reflector of dreads we can talk about, substituting flesh for dread without words. Horrors we see cover horrors we can't see. Twisted bodies divert us from our twisted souls. War physicalizes death and dread, questions the legitimacy of feelings, devalues them: it's only a feeling, a dream, something you imagined. It's not real like war. War, the great deflector of the dread we are.

*   *   *

Arnie slips from war to childhood, from childhood to war. If war physicalizes the psyche, cynicism sentimentalizes it. Cynicism and sentimentality fuse. Pity fuses with rage. War raises Arnie's consciousness and enables him to find a past stained with injury. "Already slaughtered," he muttered about himself. For periods, Arnie began many sessions crying, "Mommy, my mommy, my poor, poor mommy." From a cry it became a rant, routine, but he meant it. "All she wanted was to pour love into me, as I did with my kids." His tone made fun of his words. He could not link up enough with what he was saying but knew he was saying something real. His own children tell him he pours love into his grandchildren. "Why did I go crazy when I had children? When they had children?" Madness breaks through cynicism and sentimentality, but the latter express something too.

In many sessions there was an avalanche of negativity. "Reach out your hand and I'll chop it off," Arnie said as he walked in menacingly. Menacingly yet also collapsed, depleted, at a loss. Aggression momentarily held him together, but not very well. Hate oozed like pus from an injury, poured out like mother's love poured into him. Can one collapse from love? His voice was cynical, tinged with self-pity, accusatory. "Her love crushed my father's balls," he whispers. At first, I thought he said, "crushed my balls, her love crushed *my* balls." But no, he meant he felt castrated, depleted of power, by an overwrought sense of entitlement, over-attention, the great pouring love that he felt left his father out, left him ball-less, crushed. "And I've been a ball crusher ever since," he groaned.

Crushed, crushing. "I'd crushed your balls if they weren't already crushed," he let me know. He looked mushy rather than crushing. A mushy ghoul. Perhaps he can't bear being mushy. He tells me he is feeling bad for the bad things he has done. He can't bear how bad he's been. He confesses that if he doesn't force himself to say bad things, he would be inhibited. He talks about pushing against inhibitions, pushing an envelope. "If you don't push your envelope against inhibitions, you destroy yourself," he stammers. Is he speaking about lack of skin, needing an envelope, being suffocated by being enveloped, needing to push through?

He tells a tale of "antagonistic co-dependent" people at work who push his envelope. "They see what they can get away with, how much they can take advantage. They work enough not to get fired. Brief periods of work get them through." I get the sense he is talking about people who can't be in or out, who need to be on the brink. He is angry at them because they don't work hard and they don't leave and he can't fire them and he can't get the most out of them. Is he saying he can't break out of his mother's envelope? Did she go mad to give him space? He began his real life once she was hospitalized. If she broke down to help him, why did he break down? Their breakdowns did not seem to come from anywhere. The conclusion he was led to disgusted and appalled him: "There are seeds of madness in mother love." Mother love seeds madness? Isn't mother love good for you? Not all envelopes are too enveloping.

"You were pulverized, pushed into yourself," he glowered. The truth is I know what it is to be pulverized and pushed into yourself. He compared me to his kids who were pulverized by his wife when they were young. They learned they had to fight to survive. One had to fight cruelty and moodiness and come through. "*You* fought too. If you learn to fight early, you get used to it," he said. "You're crushed, tough, a fighter." He bemoans, again, not having to fight when he was very young. He goes over and over it. He was loved, supported, nourished – the cruelty of love. Broken, pulverized, crushed by love. Crush? Isn't that a word for love? Falling in love? Love a fall?

Undermined by love. He still expects the world to be loving and finds life hard to take, duplicitous. Life as lie, tantalizing, raising hopes, fantasy of feeling loved, then crushed. He is sick with cynicism over the fact that there is no end to disillusionment. He knows disillusionment is linked with knowledge, but it is more than he can bear. He pushes himself to fight, to have guts. He wishes he were more of a natural fighter.

Pockets of love sustain him. He repeats ad nauseam, ad infinitum, "It's hard to have an easy beginning." I wonder what is easy about any beginning. Are we going in circles? He seems to fight more than I do but sees me more as a fighter like his children, stunted fighters. He does not speak of his grandchildren as having easy lives or as fighters but they open his heart. A sense of goodness being injured touches him. More than anything, his grandchildren's vulnerability moves him, a sense of their coming through injury. He is afraid injury will mar caring. He wants them to care. He so hopes their caring will never be stunted by pain. Is this one reason he goes crazy when babies are born? He fears the pain new life must bear?

*   *   *

"Perilous . . . perilous . . ." I hear as Arnie comes in. His words are like repeating bullets under his breath. He spent the weekend in bed doing nothing. "Miraculous . . . miraculous . . . ssss . . . mmmm . . . ir . . . a. . . . Cu . . . LOUSE. . . ." he murmurs. I feel like I'm eavesdropping. I get a sense of wonder being aborted. "I'm a lifer. A lifer . . ." He means he will be in therapy for life, whether that means all his life or to get life, more life.

"I am unable to profit from experience." He means this emotionally, but he turns his head and gives me a wry stare, so that I am aware he is also referring to financial loss. He has made very bad investments over the years. Perhaps analysis is one of them.

He mentions a crisis at work, fear of people he supervises. They try to get away with as little as they can. He has to make sure things go right. The pressure is too much. Things will fall apart. He will fail and be humiliated. He feels humiliated anyway. He has to push himself to make things work. Work is important, not only because it gives him something to do, to be useful. It gives him a chance to avert destruction. The devastating outcome, the eternal peril, is miraculously sidestepped time and again.

*   *   *

"Everyone loves you," his first words through the door today. "Need people to hate. Hate feels real. Destruction feels real." He is alluding to early childhood again, the time of love, a love that stole him from himself. Does therapy, like love, constrict him? Therapy makes him feel real and unreal. He is saying that he needs life's resistance to make him feel real, whether resistance is inner or outer. He needs to push against something. He needs something to push against him. "Path of least resistance . . ." He accuses himself of taking the easy way out, part of feeling unreal. The easy way is quite hard, perilous, and involves the negative miracles of breakdowns.

"Childhood is a luxury cruise heading for an iceberg," he says, a funny twist in his voice. "It leads to feeling sorry." He is angry about good things he did this week. Can anything good come of good things? Better to be trapped in blankness, hoping only for more blankness. What good can come of goodness? Beginnings are too painful. Joy today, grief tomorrow. "I practice getting hurt to be prepared. Gorging on pain shuts it out. I'm hungry for pain, selfish pain." He drinks in mommy's pain at the breast.

"I'm mommy's puke," he says repetitively, singsong. Mommy pukes her pain into him through her breast. "My essence is puke. Pukey man . . . pukey man . . ." His is his mother's pukey pain essence. He sees her going crazy suddenly after his father died. "She puked me out," referring to birth, madness. Going mad was the only way she could get privacy, something all her own. "I did something bad," he murmurs, smearing himself with bad feelings. Therapy took a bad turn, Arnie needing to reach far into an abject core.

* * *

Father dies suddenly. Mother goes crazy suddenly. What kind of life is this? Life makes you sick. You puke it out, it pukes you out.

Someone says, "I love you." Who? Did I say it, you say it? An inside voice? Get ready to be nauseous. Something horrible is coming.

"I am mean to my wife," he says. "I feel a little bit of something, crazy with fear. She puked on the kids, I puke on her. That's what people do, puke death on each other. I love you, Michael. I wish I did. I feel a little something. I feel a little."

"I love you." What kind of love? Did I say it, did he? For a moment or two, Arnie and I inside each other inside our love, ready for life, puking madness.

* * *

Arnie takes himself off medication, feels better for a while. He wants to feel himself. He thinks he is better than five years ago when suicide was certain. In a few months bad feelings come back, mount. He tries to withstand them but fears he will not function. He fears staying in bed at weekends will spread through the week. To get through the day he goes back on medication. He does not feel much better but can do what needs to be done. After a time, he feels better but it is a better riddled with bad, sinking, ugliness. He calls it "slow suicide," years and years without sudden ending. He goes off medication again. He needs to feel raw, even for a while, like touching home. How bad can he feel? "I *am* bad," he says. He wants this to be known. Off medication he can reach abject terror. On medication he can function but, more deeply, feels despair.

Chinese box. Inside despair, mad love, inside mad love, nothingness, inside nothingness, all the feelings in the world. They thud against the medication that supports daily living. He uses medication like a soft pedal to dampen everything. He is important to too many lives. He must keep going.

*   *   *

"Trauma, trauma," he mumbles, moving towards the couch. Awash in words. "All about trauma . . . trauma . . ." It is difficult to know what he means but I believe he means something that does not stop hurting, that medication mutes but cannot end.

A switch clicks and trauma streams into sexual fissures, stinging sex, angry sex. "*Must* I fuck my children? *Must* I fuck my grandchildren?" The *must* of madness. Everyone fucks everyone but Arnie's must makes him bad. "I put my penis in a baby's mouth. I ruined a child." Before-after: his child pure and whole one moment, defiled, stained, traumatized the next. A moment one repeats over and over, form after form. A mad *must*, horrifying oneself by wounding others to show the world one's wound. To show the world that wound exists, that it must not be bypassed. Sex seizes trauma, drowns trauma, becomes trauma. What fills one with mad pleasure for a moment becomes pain forever. Arnie was driven to create infractions to house torment, sharing with others the wound he was.

A dim sense that what he did to a baby was done to him. A pleasure madness, a warp. A lonely hate called longing.

*   *   *

Arnie comes in dry weeping. *Dry weeping* are his words, like dry fucking, dry puking. He does not quite feel like weeping but gags on this non-feeling, an almost feeling. *If* he were a feeling person, weeping is what he would feel. Weeping as a feeling rather than action, although the activity counts. Fucking everywhere. Weeping everywhere. He gags on it.

He does not willfully hold back tears. There is no face for them to fall on so they do not form. They dry before they form. A word at the tip of a tongue, a tear at the tip of a soul.

"You write about self and other," he says. "I don't know anything about self and other. Cell phones are all I know about self and other." He mocks us. His cell phone rings twice and he looks to see who it is, hoping it is his special friend wanting to save him. Medication takes away libido. *Libido* is the word his doctor uses: "Medication lowers libido." What does this mean? If trauma pours into sex, and medication takes sex away, then medication takes trauma away?

* * *

He can not stop staring at the bandanna over his mother's head where they broke into her skull to make her less psychotic. He stares at her bandanna for years. He is an old man and still sees her bandanna over the marks that altered her brain. "She used to play cards. She drew, she read. She went to interesting places." He was sharing signs of intelligence, signs of life. "She took care of me." Life mattered.

Shortly before she died, he took her home. She wandered into the street and had to be brought back to the hospital. He could not take care of her. A year later, a sudden stroke and it was over. "Look how lucky I am," he mocks. "I'm psychotic too but I bounce back. I bounce through life. I won't be institutionalized. I'm a lucky psychotic, an overachieving psychotic. I work." He throws himself on the floor, writhes, clutches himself, looks at me with sheepish anguish. "I'm a screaming ghoul who can't scream. My medication provides a floor." He gets up, slouches, says teasingly, "I'll try, I'll try. I'll try again." Still dry weeping, marred.

* * *

He reminds me he is now twenty years older than his mother when she died, a kind of birthday. "I'm way out there," he says, speaking of the time line. He can not afford to be a collapsed ghoul writhing on the floor for long. He has too much responsibility. He promises to pay more attention to the ghoul's needs some day. He can not say exactly when he turned into a ghoul or how trauma soured him. A little at a time, perhaps, then some great blasts. "Someday I will find and cure it." As if one can locate the source of such pain.

He dreamt of a naked boy behind a closed door, a self left behind. "Someday I will . . ." He promised to return to his ruins and visit his nakedness.

* * *

Trauma pushed through medication but did not stop him from the chores of life. "Like a lump under psychic skin, you know it's there and your fingers keep touching it while you do other things." He gets up from the couch and glares at me, a mixture of fury and appeal, "What's the trauma, do you know?"

I almost say, "Your mother is the trauma," but he says she isn't. No need to go there again. Instead, I look at him and say, "Me, I'm the trauma. And you, you're the trauma. Having a mind like yours, a mind like mine."

He talks of people in his office. "I see traumatized beings. Its part of faces, the way a body molds around pain, tight, mushy, you see deranged areas. Deformed mind-soul-body. I feel it. Everyone must." It bothers him that people act as if no one sees things like this. One morning he woke up screaming, "No one sees things like this!"

"I've seen some people get better, some worse," he continues. "You could say I'm better some ways, worse others. Something awful goes on with no end in sight. Will it lessen if I sever with you? Do you keep it going? I broke with past therapists. I feel I can't get along without you, a false feeling. Trauma is our beings. We are it, it is us. It is not because of you or me. Are you lessening it, teaching me how to live with it, making it worse? Must I leave if I decide you are making me worse, if I'm so bad you can't help? I never felt close to past therapists. You write about closeness."

"I'm an exoskeleton," I say. "It's not your fault if we can't get close."

"No, no. Don't take the blame all on yourself. It's not so simple."

A moment of almost contact, we do feel something but we're not sure what. "I was going to say I'm perfect, kind of weird," Arnie admits. Perfect and weird. What? How? I think he means a feeling we create together as we stay with difficulties. A perfect feeling? Perhaps not, but a sense of something happening, for him, for me, perfect enough. Something sensed between us redeeming the moment. Given our problems, this feeling is its own reward. But I do not mean to stop him in his tracks. There is much to learn about being perfect. Whether weirdly perfect or perfectly weird.

* * *

"I'm not patronizing with people at work," Arnie begins, implying he's patronizing with me. "I have my father's warmth, but I'm not related. I have warmth but I don't know if I really love. I want to tell my workers I'm really crazy, take me to the hospital. I view that as progress. I know you are a good soul . . ." But powerless to help him?

He switches into a bevy of childhood scenes, rapid fire. At two riding a tricycle around a tree, round, round. Father taking him to the city to buy fish. Exposing his penis to a little girl when he was five. Trying to put it in an animal's mouth when he was eight. Playing stickball with black kids when he was ten. Wanting a camera, "the only thing I wanted." His mother got him a typewriter instead, very hard to get after the war. Baffling – why not a camera? She gave him dear things he didn't want? A madly mute frustration runs through life, mixed with pleasure, an intensity that blurs and becomes corrupt.

He goes back to where trauma comes from, draws blanks, switches gears. "*I'm* trauma." He seems to mean the advent of *I*, the process of *I'ing*. An extra plus of being, of consciousness. Mind magnifies trauma, imagination magnifies sensitivity. To imagine means to imagine oneself, to see oneself in a scene, a drama. Stops short, looks at me, asks, "Can you define what trauma is?" "Good question," I say. "There's a woman at work who makes me want to cry. I can see things happen with her, her life getting better, just amazing. She does not give up. She knows she has something to offer, something true, something to be true to. She's not corrupt. She is what I want to be, a feeling soul, a real person. I feel weepy telling you about her.

"Yesterday she caught me with my guard down, staring nowhere, not compassionate, not emotional, lost. As she was leaving she said, 'See you soon,' a warm witness. I can't tell you what it means to feel such a breath of life. She caught something in my eyes. Later I ran into her shopping. She stroked my arm, our eyes lit up.

"Look how lucky – what little pills can do. For now, anyway." Meaning he wants to come off them some day and live by eye-light. But without the pills the light might not have a chance.

Another abrupt switch, talking about strength. "Lance Armstrong – is he traumatized? Is he working out his trauma? Is it crazy to ride a bike like that?" He admires Armstrong's strength, which goes along with deprecating his own weakness. It is weak to be interested in trauma. What does trauma mean to someone like Lance Armstrong – merely something to overcome. What does it mean to Arnie? Something to be overcome by. He puts himself down, contempt for weakness. I think of him riding his tricycle around a tree when he was young, the energy, force. Where does this power go, this determination? Stuck in circles? Images of Armstrong on TV animate him. The touch and glance of a woman awaken him. He talks of other strong people, people who do things, who go from here to there, who make things happen.

"I get the sense you're searching for an area of strength to pour yourself into," I comment. "You think I can form myself around it like Lance Armstrong does?" he mocks. "Not me, buddy. All I can do is destroy life. Destroy your wife. My life – I don't know what it is." He comes close to tears, those dry tears he feels inside but do not reach the surface. "You help me, Dr. Z helps me. You lift the life of a ghoul." He needs talk therapy, he needs pill therapy, grateful for both, mocks both, mocks need.

"A ghoul, but not only a ghoul," I say, affirming what is positive about his experience. It is the wrong thing to say and aggravates him. He must prove he is no good. "I've only the trappings of family life. I'm a detached father, less of a husband. I'm still a ghoul. You write about things like this all the time." Reduction to zero.

Being touched by a woman translates, partly, into "My hero," a shift from recognition to admiration, which he attacks. Something falsifies the truth of feeling and attack tries to rectify it. It is difficult to take feeling stronger when someone graces him. A woman's touch, a rise of feeling. His mind does funny things with it, but the resonance remains. I must learn not to say anything about it. It is his within himself, within his privacy.

*　*　*

"Here is a good piece of psychotic thinking," Arnie starts. "Chocolate pop = betrayal. There's reason to it. Six years ago a doctor told my grandchild not to have chocolate, it aggravates respiratory problems. My grandchild had breathing difficulties but did not listen to the doctor and is better. My giving a pop was conspiratorial, a betrayal, risking respiratory attack. Of course, nothing happened. We enjoyed the pop. Everything was fine. But I kept thinking I betrayed the health of my grandchild. I believed I was doing something terrible, doing what the doctor said not to, even though my grandchild has been better for years. The command came from years ago. I kept hearing the word, 'betrayal.' I'm guilty, bad, I betray those I love. My grandchild would forgive me if something bad happened." So, forgiveness is in the picture, in the guilt and badness. Someone must forgive him. To be forgiven is different from forgiving. The former is addictive, the latter freeing.

He sees a new psychiatrist, different medication. Trying to find something better. His medication works but makes him feel funny. He wants a psychiatrist who cares more about the way medication feels. It's not enough to feel better, it's the way you feel better. Some ways of feeling better have a lot of worse in them. Medicine makes him more aggressive and makes his thoughts more aggressive. He wants to fuck everybody, his children, those in his care. His medicine makes him feel like someone not to trust. This morning he hasn't taken anything. Last night he took a tranquilizer and slept well. "I need pills as I don't have a psyche," he tells me. He apologizes for taking medicine, as if I'm attacking him. Taking medicine makes him feel weak. He looks down on himself for needing it. It makes him feel he will do something he shouldn't do, that he will cause harm.

"My psyche is torn. Cancer, metastasized. I'll take a pill so I can get through the day. I need to function. It makes me feel dangerous but also enables me to act like a human being. I shouldn't have done it, given the chocolate pop. It was a dangerous thing to do, a wrong thing.

"Thou shalt not eat chocolate," I say. Sweet, dark. The list of things he shouldn't have done.

"I go to see my children looking for radiance," he says. He feels remorse to right things. Remorse balances radiance. Both are crucial.

* * *

Arnie speaks of a trauma clot. Our being together helps bits of it break off and dissolve into his psychic bloodstream. The clot is endless. It blocks breathing. It creates tension. He squeezes himself around it but it does not give way, not fully. He must live with it, although he does not stop chipping away at it. The clot holds a lot of pain that can not be suffered. It is, partly, made up of hatred of pain, a contraction. Sometimes Arnie feels that he is in the clot and that it is pinching him, suffocating him. There is something strangulated about trauma. Mutilated, mangled are other words. They point to a great deformity, a blockage. Is there any life without it? Arnie no longer knows. He lives in the places he can. He has done much better than his parents, than all his immediate, familial predecessors. In one or another way, he survives himself. He knows that chocolate is good and that he and his grandchild will survive its murderous sinfulness. They will survive what is bad. The fact is he bought chocolate pops and they had a good time eating them, even if he had to withstand a taste of hell. His grandchild will grow and Arnie's love will grow. You tell me he could be doing better? He and I say, we are doing what we can.

Notes

1. I've written about the heh-heh devil in a number of places, particularly in *The Psychotic Core* (1986) and *The Electrified Tightrope* (1993, Chapter 16, "Demonized Aspects of the Self"). In *The Psychotic Core* I describe a malignant, transcendent mental self which mocks and denigrates a semi-mesmerized, alternately passive-explosive body self. I believe this to be a widespread structure of our times.

2. Freud (1921) writes of a transference madness in everyday life, in which leaders and authorities of various kinds are idealized and over-estimated, often with disastrous results. In extreme, but not uncommon instances, we look for individuals or groups to fulfil a messianic function (Bion, 1970).

CHAPTER FIVE

Election Rape

"Y ou will think I'm paranoid but I can't help putting together the way Bush stole the election and 9/11." Carla was referring to the presidential election year 2000. "They bullied, lied, cheated on every level. Blocking voters from voting: getting voters off the lists, creating obstacles getting to polls, creating problems at the polls, bad ballot forms, bad ballot counts, discrediting credentials . . . Bullying. Baker's face bore a hole through me. I had nightmares about his face and Pataki shouting at vote counters in Florida. No wonder I was turned off by politics when I was a teen.

"I feel raped by the Supreme Court! What do kids learn from the Supreme Court? They learn to do anything to win, screw others to get power. Lie and cheat and bully. Not only is being a rapist OK, it's mandatory. It's part of what one does to win. May the best rapist win. At Bush's inauguration the streets were lined with the violated.

"They bombed us with the election, then 9/11 came. I thought: violence to violence, mirror images, violence trapped in a magnification lens. Monster, monster on the wall, who's the evilest of all? There is a grotesque mirror in the soul and once you fall in you can not get out of it.

"Rape spreads.

"A month to Halloween. There were no parties. A year later I dressed as a prophet: 'Woe, woe. Where is repentance?' 9/11 silenced me. I breathed ash. You couldn't hear traffic. What stuck to the magnet of my mind: Enron, Halliburton, the California energy rip-off. Corporate rape, the Bush team trying to rip off Alaskan oil, screw California, screw the environment, tax breaks for the wealthy, milk the world.

"Terrorist chatter didn't get through because their heads were filled with economic noise. Acting like they're right, like they *are* America, the American people this, the American people that . . . Well, I'm an American people and I *don't* want what they want. They sure as hell don't speak for me.

"I didn't know so many felt as I did until the march [before the 2004 Republican convention in New York City]. The immensity of the outpouring: so many different kinds of people with the same sense of violation. Togetherness inside the rape."

Carla was abused by an uncle in childhood. From earliest memory, he penetrated her with tongue, hand, genitals. He began when she was an infant. I would not be surprised to learn he was mouthing and fingering her genitals or touching her with his penis before she was six months old. He was part of her life before she could speak. One can only imagine what it was like for her to come into language with him part of it. She grew into language with him inside her organs of speech.

Carla has dim memories of a woman's voice, likely her mother's saying, "No, that's not right." A man saying, "It's OK. She likes it." Voices inside a moist feeling, mouth tonguing, speaking inside genitals. She lying on her back in a crib, not knowing what was doing what. A man's mouth doing something she could not see. Yet she knew precisely. She knew exactly what he was doing and why. Uncanny clarity fused with not knowing, clarity and confusion penetrating her being, remaining all her life. Rounded by outside sensations, hard face, scratchy whiskers, soft mouth, a round, fuzzy, insistent sense of shared surfaces.

A pattern of ignoring what was happening and making believe she did not know what captured her attention, was in place before she spoke. Memory? Imagination? A moist, warm, rough sensory stain soaking words. Clara relates scraps of events lodged in her, like gunshot in inoperable wounds healing over invasive material. The word healing: a misnomer when it comes to psychic wounds in one's body, the atmosphere of speech, the tone and cast of sound and color.

Fantasy weaves webs of feelings. Carla's mother fails to act. Her objection subsides. Woman succumbs. Violation is part of the fabric of life. Woman gives birth. Man creates realities babies grow up in. *"She likes it – it's OK."* *What* is it she likes? Does she even know? Moist warmth feels OK. Does she like it or not? Can there be an *or*? What is *it*? Does the idea of liking make sense? It is more or other than liking, something more difficult, complex, tantalizing. The tickling slips under, then away from liking, pleasurable, powerless. The pleasure of power slips away. She lies without protection, something happening inside the helplessness. *She* is being defined by what he does. And if she is being marked as a passive subject, there is a lot going on in the passivity, a lot of transgressive activity. Triangles in her nerves: she done to; man the doer; a concerned, failing mother as onlooker. To be a doer, be a man. To be done to, a woman. But *who* is done to, who looks on? There is muddled, persistent curiosity: what is happening to *me*? what is *this*? A mind pressing for birth. There are times violation excites subjective presence, subjective invagination with gripping insistence.

In Freud's writings, uncle turns out to be father. Could father do this in front of mother, sexually violate daughter while mother says no? A violation of mother's no. What can yes and no mean to a girl from this point on? More is at stake than sensation. Sensation is part of a field of pleasure fused with power, a play of desire and will. Abdication and helplessness play a major role. Women flutter around male force.

But it is not only force. Something lascivious clings to the skin, something perverse. Henceforth it is only anal sex that gives Carla satisfaction. By the time she was three or four, probably before, she spent hours finding new ways to masturbate her anus. "It was the one hole he didn't find," she said. "It was something all my own." This, of course, was illusion, hallucination: to hallucinate a hole all one's own. Her uncle-father long ago took possession of it. Perhaps what she experienced was taking possession of his possession: of herself as his possession, of him as possessor of herself, while remaining elusive as transcendental onlooker biding time. There is no place like the asshole to hide and wait and exert uncanny control invisibly.

The political scene becomes a place to read what happened as a baby. Violation writ large. Not just an infant or little girl in the privacy of family but in broad daylight in front of a nation. Rape and rip-off for all to see. A magnified parallel to her situation as a baby, plundered by father in front of mother. A scene of plunder while an audience looks on, perhaps semi-mesmerized by force and cunning, paralysis induced by disbelief or by some difficult to grasp unconscious fascination.

One factor in the brew is reversal: repaint a situation to favor a particular point of view: *my* will, desire, right, pleasure, power over yours, even *as* yours. An example is: *"She* likes it," when neither liking nor disliking is the salient point. The baby hears herself referred to as she, third party, her subjectivity treated from outside as if the outsider had inside access. As if he were more inside her than she. "She likes it" threatens to be a defining truth about experience. Whether or not liking – her liking – rises to relevance or whether she even knows about her liking. The knowing of the other substitutes for her knowing, threatens to become what she knows. The other's evaluation of her insides threatens to be her insides. The other's insides slides into hers with a tingling, eerie sense that something wrong is happening.

It is not the deepest knowing, not the deepest inside to inside contact, but deep enough. There is something off in the father's way of defining her reality, not only from outside but from above, a kind of sick Mosaic law: Thou shalt like . . . *it*, what I do, what I say you like. Thou shalt become a she that likes my sick law. Something tricky, snaky (up her ass), greedy (usurping baby's hunger), self-oriented (substituting for the baby's right to have her moment): she likes it because I want her to, because I want to think she likes it. Now you see why we invent God as spirit, omniscient, unencumbered by body: because there is direct, immediate mind to mind influence, I to I influence. What I like, she likes. It is not only that difference is obliterated. I–I, mind–mind transmission happens over it, under it, through it, to a side. Hostile, corrupt magic (hostile takeover): my wish is her wish. As if she is in his power in his mind. Wishing becomes willing and willing makes it so.

One source of confusion and paralysis is collapse of ability to locate herself outside the other's desire, which includes an imaged assessment of her desire. Another thread of paralyzed confusion is the surreptitious seeing of the other's will and desire gliding into oneself. One watches suspended as the gliding will defines, ignores, uses what it finds. One is fascinated by the discovery of permeability and psychic transfer, watching it at work with the passive fullness of watching movies, movies of one's insides taken over by another's. One realizes that separation is no barrier. Everything depends on the quality of entry and permeability.

What gets lost but not lost is the sense that what is happening is wrong. An implicit sense of justice: this is not right, this is off, yet one does not know what to do about it. What *can* one do about it? Scream? Cry? Withdraw? Strike out? Relax and enjoy it? Succumb? One is not sure of the meaning of what is happening, so what is happening is thrown into question. One is not sure how to evaluate it. One lies there, partly in perplexity, waiting, tasting medleys of sensations and mute thoughts, not able to sort things out. One is, partly, waiting for things to get clear, take shape. One is waiting for help, transparency, visibility.

Meanwhile, complex tensions form. Thinking is affected. Mixtures of blankness, swirls and peaks, suspicion, obsession, hysteria, splitting off. A feeling of something wrong buried by continued growth.

I don't think the wrong thing goes away. Often anger sticks to it and in some cases, destruction writ large. Normally, we limp along, skip along, learn to live with our strengths and weaknesses. We get along and do well enough. Carla lived a decent life. But as she moved into her forties, she feared missing something. She also felt haunted. Missing and haunted were not the same. Her pleasure had been work, leisure, travel, affairs, some longer relationships. Work organized her life. Now time scared her. She imagined she would have children some day but that day escaped her. Her life had been good enough to ignore wrong, missing, haunted things.

One day when I was pressing Carla to say more about missing and haunted, she spontaneously burst out, "I feel filled by anal sex. Yet I hide. No one can find me. I am safe inside my asshole. I divert attention from myself, fill myself without showing. I like it from behind, unseen. No one can see me. I am invisible. They can't have *me* but I have them, they fill me. I can surrender without surrendering. I have everything without giving very much." A feed without acknowledging the reality of the feeder. It is enough to be filled by an organ. Saturated, orgasmic, blank sex. The tie with fecundity is broken, free from generational chains. Yet she misses what generational chains can give. She has swallowed up, supplanted babies she might have had by a rear fill, a passage no real babies traverse. It is not unusual to substitute one hole for another. A fantasy may be to plug all leaks, completion, fill all lacks, but then the living not-me of a child is lacking. A great not stays stuck inside, unborn.

The haunting is something gone wrong: father as signifier/purveyor of basic rape, violation of self and deformation of personality one tries not to notice. Did father cause it, express it, both? Isn't violation primordial, awaiting the person, ready to take different forms? Waiting for one to grow into it? Clara's father may be Violation with a Thousand Faces, yet be a special trauma point, a privileged inflictor, a particularly scathing trauma bearer.

Clara now feels violation coming at her from political events. Strong violation she partly organizes herself around. "They lied. They lied. They knew Iraq had no weapons of mass destruction. They ignored expert advice. They slanted things the way they wanted. Reality is what *they* say. It doesn't matter what *we* say." A fit between politics and childhood trauma. Abuse covered by befuddlement, excusing the abuser. Violation counts on oblivion. It's hard to believe what's happening actually is happening. It's hard to believe it *could* happen.

Outrage at violation and abuse is played on, obscured, diverted, re-channeled, as children, as adults. You want to think well of your father, your leader, your government, your courts of appeal. As a child and citizen you look for excuses, whitewash what's wrong. Too often perpetrators feel right, even righteous or, at least, play on confusion about reality that leaders organize. Right and wrong reverse and reverse again. Sometimes perpetrator and victim reverse, each carrying on scenarios of the other through generations. Reversal and rigidity go together.

There is a fit between Carla's experience of the world in adulthood and violation she carried from infancy. Beneath or within traumatized oblivion and confusion is an abiding sense of injustice, something wrong. A sense of right and wrong on an emotional level, violation of sensitivity. It may get pummeled, reversed, displaced, diffused, re-channeled, but it does not simply end. It disturbs sleep, disturbs dreams, obscurely haunts one's days. Something wrong that haunts existence. A sense of violation that travels through life, perhaps is constitutive. Not just something external to being, that should not, might not be there, but part of the way we are given to ourselves. Violation as part of physical and psychological birth, part of originating processes, processes that make us up, make us possible. Election rape, economic rape, military rape, familial rape.

We perpetuate and elaborate violence through symbols and actions that have symbolic meaning. We attack Iraq because we have been attacked by Al Qaeda. We attack Iraq because we *can*. It is something we can get away with – or think we can get away with, under-estimating or not really caring about the human cost. It matters more that we attack than whether we are aiming at the right enemy. The enemy will come soon enough. A kind of variation of the build and they will come idea: destroy and they will come.

To attack Iraq in response to being attacked by Al Qaeda makes a kind of sense. Iraq and Al Qaeda meld in many American minds ("they're all the same") and, in any case, displacement is part of the way psychic processes work. Apparently, the difference between a terrorist network and local tyrant was too tough a discrimination to maintain. The difference between liberals (anything goes) and conservatives (moral values) was easier.

Who attacks who matters to us: to us power matters. To history, it almost seems, who does what to who matters less than x is done. For example, subject and object reverse or change around a violent link. Violence remains the same, while who's doing it to whom varies. The need to violate persists through changing scenarios and drama-tis personae. Destruction is contagious and spreads from subject to subject. Where does it start? Where do we find an origin? Rape of children? Of childhood souls? Isn't violence already in place await-ing the birth of more subjects? We have a lust for origins. We trace our violent nature back to a Big Bang, to an explosive beginning, a continuity between explosive processes in nature and us. If we are an ongoing part of partly violent processes, it is not surprising to find that the way we govern ourselves is not violence free.

Yet there is another vision, another thread. We have a prophetic, ethical dimension, a profound sense that we ought not injure one another. Not only a demand from without, but a real caring, part of the way we love. A sense that we are precious, worth the effort.

We don't know how to connect the dots between our violent and caring natures. Perhaps there are no dots to connect. Both tendencies are deeply rooted in our beings. We learn that it is impossible not to injure ourselves and each other. Experiences like forgiveness and reparation grow around the sense of injury. There are moments of grace when goodness blossoms of itself. One also needs to learn that a certain amount of opposition to oneself is necessary.

Ancients tell us to strike a balance but we are uncertain what the balance is. William Blake tells us we know we've gone too far when we've gone *much* too far – Enough or Too much. He meant it positively, but there is something in us that may not realize we've tipped a pot of boiling oil over, even after we are scalded and others are burnt beyond recognition. There is an oblivion that surrounds our will, cloaks us until we go as far we can, until we win, or until damage we endure and cause creates sufficient outcry.

We can't eradicate destructiveness, but aren't some rapes avoidable? Isn't education supposed to help extend ourselves, if necessary struggle with ourselves?

What will it take to learn to minimize destruction? There is no substitute for self-struggle, not just a superficial reining in, but radical critique of our make-up.

We are experimenting with what is possible and what is possible changes. Psychotherapists, a marginal group, try to listen and respond. We hear private outcry, private outrage that spans dimensions: familial, biological, cultural. People are outraged by deformations they have undergone in response to pressures exerted by their own personality. They hate the kind of persons they have become. Some feel boxed in or crushed by physical trauma, upbringing, cultural mayhem and coldness. We are a land of opportunities, but the tradeoffs can be grave. It would be delusional to think the little good we do with some people can make a dent in the immensity of problems that beset the world. But I am not convinced our work is entirely without effect.

Meanwhile, I listen to Clara speak about her asshole. It is a delicate, if crude topic and I feel a little like I'm eavesdropping. She does not show embarrassment and I loosen up. She speaks of anal rape and does a double take: "Is anal rape possible? Not for me. And yet – I do feel I mimic rape, undo rape, make it good."

Make bad good. Something awful left a stain she tries to wash out by re-creating the negative more positively. A taste of heaven in her asshole, where her orgasms hide out. She confided a number of times, "You know, anal sex is heavenly." On several occasions she added – "a heavenly violation." My vision: heavenly violation inscribed in flesh trying to wash horrific violation out of soul. For moments of pounding, she succeeds, near-ecstasy moments, full, saturated. The stain reforms and she must undo it again. To make the bad thing go away for awhile, to bang violation away is a reprieve. She has hit on a use of body or fantasy body that nullifies violation with an act that once violated her, a channel that transforms violation into pleasure. Fight fire with fire: anal ecstasy blisses out anal rape.

She brings her hurting soul to therapy, pain without an ending. There is need for a lot of sorting out. "Positive and negative assholes," she puts it. A creative asshole aware of anal violation. "One reason I came to you was your expertise in anal devils. You write about anal devils. All the sayings about getting it from behind, sneak attack, tricky mind. Sometimes you look like an anal devil. I have a joyous ass. You have a tight ass. You're also a playful devil. You don't talk me out of my asshole things.

"I never really felt the right to be alive. I fuck to make believe I'm alive. I look at men and think, can they pound the shit out of me? Shit equals everything wrong, all my damage, all the damage in the world. I want a fucking cure. In South America I spent hours watching women pound clothes on rocks in water, making the soul of the clothes clean. I pound my asshole soul clean but shit is self-replenishing.

"Terrorists tried to clean the world by taking a giant shit on the World Trade Center, wiping it away. The Bush network shit on the country, wiping away an election, then shit on Iraq to clean the mess." Cleaning by shitting on: a psychosocial wipe-out operation. Shitting on as a form of rape and vice versa. Carla's language slips between shitting and raping, and shitting-raping across micro-macro spheres, individual, familial, economic, political. A language of violence and spoiling, part of a trauma language.

Rape irradiates, networks of trauma nodes gravitate towards each other. There is a resonance in Clara's life between childhood and world trauma. As a little girl, rape dissolved in daily life. As an adult, it screams in world events. Clara makes contact with childhood rape through national rape. She regains part of her trauma history by sensitivity to world events, by her rage at history. In her personal life, Clara covered trauma with pleasure and personal sat-isfaction. A good asshole covers a lot of sins. Personal satisfaction is important. But there is a point past which no sweet ass can hide the abuse that taints the smell of social-political life.

Lies lighten public violation, put good names on bad things. Rape becomes an atmospheric condition. Lies of leaders almost work like a mommy saying, "All better," so patriotic children no longer feel the open wound. But there are points where bullying and sneakiness rupture the shell. Disgust and horror obtrude. Trauma leaks. Destructive use of power comes out in the open. Damaged depths of one's own being rise to meet it. It is this juncture, stirring, outpouring of the awful that drives Carla to see me, to seek what is true in her life, to seek what is necessary.

Wounds hide in disbelief. We can't believe this happened, is hap-pening, that such things can be. The traumatizing aspect of power counts on the time lapse between disbelief and horror, between the horror that leads to disbelief, and the horror that awakens realization of one's condition.

CHAPTER SIX

Healing Longing

ad girl, lonely, living by herself at the moment. She had to wait three weeks to see me and called five times after making the appointment. I didn't think she'd show up.

And here she was. I think, "My God, she got here!"

It's hard to hear. There are a lot of street noises and she speaks quietly. I move my chair a little closer. Her face is pasty, pressed in, sensitive. I'm tempted to say embryonic but that is too hasty. The pressed in quality, not pinched exactly, exercises me. I wait on it.

She loves her previous therapist, a woman she saw over ten years. Her therapist left to become a mother. She said she'd practice again in a few months, which became half a year, a year, longer. Eventually, it was obvious her therapist was working, but not with her.

Annette's calls, hundreds eventually, went unanswered. The few times she got through, her therapist hung up on her. Once, before hanging up, she told Annette directly and coldly, "I gave you someone's name. Call *her*."

I felt pained for Annette, worried and stymied. What to think? What to believe? Thoughts ran through my mind – was Annette too much for a new mother? Too needy, too many calls, threats? Things change when you have a baby. When I became a father, I slept in sessions, dropped things, came up with odd ideas. I felt I was fuller, caring. Fatherhood brought me to new places, including an insistent sense that we were all parents and children to one another. But I was also out of it much of the time.

Annette was sure that it was not caring that motivated her therapist's getting rid of her. Eventually, caller ID screened her out and she wrote letters, letter after letter.

"Dear X – I can't tell you how much you mean to me. Our work saved my life. I know I'm not a good patient. I promise to try harder. I'll talk about things that are important and make better use of what you offer. Please talk to me."

She told me she used to injure herself, that she had been hospitalized many times for depression, including suicide attempts and urges. She feared she would sink underneath again, that she was close. She was nearing fifty and endured these states since her teens. I began to marvel at the insistent strength of illness. She looked like a will of the wisp, ready to be blown over, lifted away with a wind. She was too "weak" to hold a normal job, never had a love relationship (except with her therapist) – yet somehow fed off the strength and persistence of depressive longing. Can depression make one strong?

I began wondering, "Ah, that pressed in look – yes, it's crushed, definitely ingrown, contracted – but a dense strength hides in it. That pasty quality with an amorphous touch – a little like mud that endures, becomes sand, becomes clay, becomes rock."

So that is the feeling that comes through, with more weight than I first imagined, "My God, she's here!"

* * *

I knew from the outset I did not have time to see her, not the time she needed. And she did not have money to pay me. What money her father had left was nearly gone. Her mother died long before. She asked me to see her for free, but I did not want to do that. My time is pretty filled and I have kids to support through school. But she kept calling and now and then we met. She said she liked being with me. We seemed to be comfortable together, talking or not talking as the spirit moved us. More deeply, she was too afraid to say a lot of what she felt. I guess she felt more comfortable being uncomfortable with me than with others she tried. Or maybe I was the only one who tolerated her calls.

She was on a lot of medication, looked after by a psychiatrist, the most recent of a line of doctors who came and went. I get the sense that she had seen workers at the start of their practice, who then dropped her as they moved on. During the day she read, helped the homeless, dropped in to a part-time day program, donated time to inpatients. She was productive with her time but did not make money. For a time, her calls to me increased. Once I said, "You probably don't realize you called me twenty times in a twenty-four period. Maybe you were just in your head, in your anxiety, in your desperation, and lost track of the times you pressed my number." I know she tried to hold herself back from flooding my life. But she let on she knew that was one reason why her therapist kicked her out.

There was no way I could take her as a full time patient. For a few moments near the beginning, I thought of reducing my fee but decided against it. With all the calls and emails, I decided to keep my fee high enough so as not to resent the intrusion. Catch-22: that meant she could not see me often, so the cycle of intermittent visits continued, with calls and emails and letters. Intrusion, bombardment, flooding, outpouring. Annette submerged in her fluctuating states, impelled to share them, to announce them, a sportscaster from hell, saying what it is like to go from fire to fire, the latest news off an emotional ticker-tape.

Why did I continue to see her? At first I thought I'd tide her over until she got started with someone else – provide a net while she re-grouped. But the net got stretched very thin. Months went by and she'd accumulate funds for a session. "You know," I told her. "I don't listen to most of your calls. There are just too many. I wish I could but I simply can't. But I do sample them and I know they communicate pretty much the same feeling. You are unhappy your old therapist won't see you. It is a loss that feels like the loss of your parents, your mother when you were young. You need to tell me, tell someone, tell everyone how bad it feels, how lonely and unhappy you are, how afraid you are that you are sinking, that you want me or someone to pull you up." I think the fact that I don't listen to many of her calls or see her often makes it possible to maintain contact. But a sub-voice, maybe common sense, says, "You're stopping her from seeing someone else. If you cut off, maybe she'd find someone."

Nevertheless, we continued. We felt a feeling together. An appeal, suffering, lonely longing, hoping, despair. But more, an inside chest feeling linked to skin, to eyes. I liked to look at her and she liked to look at me.

I feared doing her an injustice. By this time I learned that her loss of her past therapist was not an isolated incident. None of her therapies had a happy ending. This last therapist was the only one she loved. It sounded like Annette got led on for years, but in the moment things feel differently. I feared the leading on feeling was coming about again and my sub-voice warned, "This feeling is a link that's bound to recoil." A feeling in my chest would rise and touch something similar in her, and I could not say a final no.

*   *   *

One day she came in clutching an article she found in my waiting room saying, "Is this what we're doing? Surrendering to each other?" My waiting room is filled with books and papers. The one in her hand was Emmanuel Ghent's (1990) 'Masochism, submission, surrender'. She reads to me of a longing, a wish, an impulse to surrender that heals wounds, creates something new. It is a revelation. That is what she wants, what she wanted with her earlier therapist. But things always go wrong: aborted surrender sinks into endless damage.

"I'm not sure my problem is masochism, submission or things Ghent lists (compliance, false self, sadism), but something more drastic, more deadly. More pervasive. My whole personality is messed up. *I'm* messed up. I don't exactly see me mirrored in his article but I see my longing mirrored." A longing for healing deep in the damage. Maybe a damaged longing too, but a longing that has a healing hope.

Can longing heal damage? Is it the result of damage? When I'm with Annette, I realize the longing she has does not fit the way I feel. It's closer to the way I felt years ago before my life took hold. I suppose it could return and Annette is a reminder. I've gotten busy, strong, involved, put together through love of family and work. Too much to do to be devoured by destructive longing. There, I've said it: destructive longing. I've made a pairing: destructive and creative longing. I've bounced into Ghent's world, surrender vs submission, masochism, false self, compliance, sadism – perversions of the real coin.

We're on a long, twisted path, hard to get off. Walls grow up around this path as we walk, sealing escape. I'm tempted to sit and wait, take out a drill, look for a weak spot, sneak another try, another spot.

"Controlling," Annette says. "My therapist said I was trying to get into her life, take over her life. She said she understood, that I was in pain and would get better. She would be there, we would work it out in time, I would grow.

"That didn't happen. I stayed the same and she didn't want to be with me. She called me controlling. I felt desperate. With my *head*, I *know*, I *see* that when I call you fifty times it's controlling, but I feel I'm looking for a response. I feel desperation. My therapist taught me clinging makes me controlling. Clinging is controlling. But what does it control? Am I trying to control you and her or am I trying to get a hold on, stop from going under, stop a final disappearance?

"*That* is what I feel, desperate disappearance. Clinging to life looks controlling. Like grabbing a hand in water over my head and I can't swim, paralyzed, and the other gets afraid and struggles to get away to save themselves. I'm someone people need to get away from. There is an unbearable gap between what I feel inside and how I feel to others.

"Ghent would know. He wouldn't be afraid. He'd recognize I'm a perversion of myself, a negative image, that good stuff was there seeking light, seeking growth. That the bad stuff was the good stuff in disguise, messed up, crushed."

Should I call Mannie and warn him Annette might call? No, he can take care of himself. What is important is her image and sense of Mannie now, in the moment that we speak. Through the article she heard someone who hears. She felt a twinge of recognition. Is this purely imaginary, did something real come through?

* * *

"I love her and she loves me," declared Annette. It was rock bottom certainty, psychic fact, a nucleus of her being. She was certain her therapist loves her, not just loved her. Love – present tense. Love at the center of being, the heart of life.

At the same time she was swimming, sinking, falling apart, lost. Disappearing. Abandoned, rejected. When she is dropped she shatters. Disappears. When she is cared for she comes back. Re-appears. Love puts her together. Rejection kills.

It will not do to say, "You are too sensitive. Toughen up. Everyone has to learn to deal with rejection, loss, lack. You too, no exceptions. Get with the program."

She wants her feelings recognized. She wants what she goes through to be honored, memorialized. I think of the Viet Nam Memorial, Holocaust memorials, the memorial in process for the World Trade Center. She wants her pain, shatter, disappearance memorialized. I will walk in the museum of her psyche, landmark of pain and injury, and pay respects.

At the center of shatter, love. Love at the point of disappearance. Crushed, numbed, paralyzed – but in its own way, love.

A feeling that someone loves me in the hate, that I love through my misery. I am decimated, but not without love, I'm decimated because I'm loveless. Does love hide lovelessness? Does lovelessness hide from love? Are both defensive? Are both rock-bottom? There is no way out of this.

Can we get into it more?

* * *

"Surrender and controlling don't go together," says Annette. "In Ghent they are foils. They take one to different places. Surrender opens, controlling closes. Life isn't neat. Very controlling people make discoveries, the need to control fuels learning. What would we accomplish if we just stayed open all the time?"

"You mean, surrender and controlling make a couple, a pairing?" I say.

Control in service of surrender, surrender in service of control.

"We need both," she continues. "We *are* both. I'm not sure about either. I know I'm controlling but don't feel it. I see it and believe it but can't contact it. Misery is what I feel. Desperation. I feel I am disappearing. Perpetual disappearance. That is my being. My reality. What my therapist called controlling is me trying to put the brakes on. To slow the disappearance. To keep disappearance at a slower speed – you can't stop it. All the "controlling" in the world can't stop it. The controlling grows from disappearing. To stop "controlling," I'd have to stop disappearing. You can't make disappearing disappear. Disappearing is who I am. Disappearing shatters. Disappearing is part of shatter. Shatter never stops. A kind of disappearing shatter, shattering disappearance. It's beautiful when it's fireworks and you want it to go on forever. But when it is your self, you want it to stop.

"At first I thought surrender would make it stop, that surrender means disappearing altogether. It's comforting to think about surrender. You let all the misery go. You open up and it goes. I don't think I do this. I hold on. But I think it. Wish it. Is surrender a wish? Can it be real?

"Ghent makes it sound like a dream, a dream I'd like to be in. I want to say he makes it real, but I can't say that. It sticks where I'm stuck. Incessant shatter. I want shatter to become surrender.

"Maybe surrender means disappearance of self. Finally, free. The disappearing finally completes itself. I'm aborted disappearance. Disappearance can't complete itself. It can never be fulfilled. Surrender seems fulfilling. Ghent says that submission transforms into its positive. Maybe disappearance can too. Maybe disappearance can transform into surrender, at least a tiny bit.

"I'm too sick for submission. Too far gone for masochism. Is Ghent talking about more cohesive people, more put together sick people? I think sadism and masochism make you feel whole, make you feel unitary. My therapist thought I was masochistic to myself, sadistic to her. If she's right, I don't *feel* it. What I feel is sickness, *me*, something wrong with *me*. It's not like I'm masochistic, submissive. Ghent talks about seeking pain. I *am* pain. *I* am pain. My *I* is a rotten tooth, a rotting nerve. The idea of surrender is tormenting. I don't know if he has room for sick people like me. It sounds like he's not talking about people as bad as I am.

"Who surrenders to what? Who to who? I said we surrender to each other, but is that true? Maybe I gave the wrong name to something I felt, something I thought *we* felt. You're not even my therapist. You don't have time. I don't have money. What *are* we doing? I come, you see me. What *is* this? I don't think it is surrender, is it? *Something* gets touched. We get into what we get into. It's never enough. But I feel better after I leave – for a while. I feel better telling you how bad things are."

* * *

It feels timeless. Perhaps not quite, not exactly. As if time were an agony and we meet in different parts of the agony.

Annette has been living with Ghent's paper, next to her bed when she sleeps and wakes up, on subway rides between activities. He has become part of her internal conversation. She called him several times and hung up without speaking. She knew he wouldn't see her.

Couldn't help her. Would it be worse if he could? It was a fantasy. She couldn't pay his fee. Why start another disappearing situation. To see someone who had to disappear. To say she was addicted to disappearance is too weak. She *is* disappearance. She *is* what she fears. A kind of Midas, everything she touches disappears.

But she holds on to the article. Her bare room is papered with it. Its pages multiply when she sleeps. While she makes breakfast, it becomes a plant that sprouts all around her, covers her eyes. An Emmanuel Ghent plant, pages everywhere. His words cover her, shield her ears, a quiet voice that protects her, makes her a little better.

"Ghent says its irrelevant who or what you surrender to, the surrendering process is what's important. I'd like to surrender to someone who will be there, who stays, who doesn't disappear. Whenever I start to open, the other leaves. That's my experience, my life. Ghent talks about something beyond that, opening to life that is such an opening that it encompasses disappearance. An opening that opens you to another place, where the opening itself is enough.

"An opening to true self, he says. Is he assuming there is a true self? Is the true self undamaged? Nothing escapes damage. My life, my being, my personality is damaged through and through. Where can trueness come from? There's no place for it.

"Church spoiled Jesus for me when I was a little girl. But now I see the agony and maybe truth is in the damage. I don't know how that works. Cruelly, I suppose. I can't imagine. Truth is in the damage. But what is all this true self talk? It sounds like a cruel fantasy to torture sick people like me.

"He quotes someone – a Marion Milner[1] do you know of her? – about a growth force, a fury to grow, 'a kind of creative fury.' I wish I had that. That doesn't seem like me at all. Can that happen for me? It seems remote. The air has been let out of my life. My life sinks, collapses. There's not much left to me. Just enough to keep disappearing.

"I'm in obliteration mode. That's my big discovery. I've fallen into obliteration. It leaves just enough of me to keep on feeding it. I'm an obliteration farm. Enough of me is grown by an evil being to feed an obliteration machine. Can Ghent stomach this kind of malignancy. Would he see my malignancy as aborted growth asking for help? What can be done?

"Doesn't there have to be more of a person, more health, for surrendering? If all you see is Chinese boxes of sickness, endless, holographic sickness – what can surrendering do, where can it come from? In such a poisoned, twisted world can there be anything but poisonous, twisted surrender? I can't meditate, I can't sit – all the bad stuff, the nightmare, it's too scary to sit with myself. But I can sit here for a while. Painful, still. I sit quietly wanting to tell you more. If you weren't here, I couldn't bear this. I couldn't do this. I would die and go under. That is what it's like all the time, dying and going under. You think it would have to stop but it doesn't stop. Ghent makes it sound so benign. But what about people like me?

"There's something good in his voice. Something I believe, that gets through to me. Like the love I feel, the love my therapist and I have for each other. She kicked me out. She won't see me. She won't answer may calls or my letters. She does not want me in her life. How can our love be real?

"But I feel it *is* real. I believe it. How can that be? I don't know. I'm glad it's there. It is all that is meaningful. It is hope. It isn't surrender. It *fills* surrender. It substitutes for surrender. It *fills* me – when I feel it. Can she take it away by rejecting me? Can she make it go away? She can make it painful, she can shake it. It is like a light you keep blowing on and it keeps going on. You can't make it go out, not a final out. Tell me it's a make believe real love, but it's all I have left.

"I think the truth is I feel the rise of love when someone is kind to me. My therapist tried to help me so many years before she got tired of it. I can feel she cared. When I see you are patient and listening I am tempted to think this is love. What it probably is is someone being nice to me. I'm that starved, that empty, that needy. Someone being nice makes love come.

"I doubt I'll ever get as far as surrender. Can love be part of surrender, surrender part of love? Ghent's paper excludes me. A positive world I'll never get to. Yet his voice touches me. I'm not totally outside of it. A taste comes through."

* * *

I think a lot about Annette between sessions. Maybe there is an extra edge of love for those she can not have. I don't hear much about love when she talks about people she helps or people who might not reject her. I've suggested clinics and therapists she could work with, but she finds reasons not to go. The biggest stated reason is that she doesn't want to be with someone who will leave her again. But I've begun to suspect that is exactly what she needs to reproduce.

She keeps dropping in on me, although she knows she can't really be my patient. She imagines our intermittent contacts provide some protection against opening up and being left, but it also animates a sense of never having, always leaving. Perhaps having a little.

It took her years to begin opening up with her past therapist. Throughout their time together, she felt she wasn't doing what she was supposed to do. She wasn't being a good patient, talking about her feelings. When she was in sessions, she fell silent. She didn't have feelings to talk about. She became anxious, tongue-tied, and counted on her therapist's patience. She blamed herself for not getting anywhere. Her therapist seemed to blame her too. Annette wanted therapy to make the bad feelings go away. Instead, she was stymied, a frustrating burden on her therapist and herself.

Is she right that she is not organized enough for submission, compliance, false self? Her letters to her therapist were abject, sometimes blaming. They accused her therapist of lacking fidelity, for leaving, as if therapy promises more, perhaps more than it can deliver. They excuse her therapist for leaving, given what a failure as a patient Annette was.

Can therapy deliver fidelity? Must it end in betrayal? Annette's therapies fail to come through the sense of betrayal that is one thing therapy deals with. Therapy tries to negotiate states like betrayal. Therapy is not pure and it impurely works with its impurities. I get the sense that Annette wants pure love. She wants love to be pure – therapy love to be pure and enduring. Her unending demand for therapy love may be one factor that unnerved her therapist, who must have discovered that in the battle between love and disappearance, love tended to disappear.

Annette's pleading and begging looked a lot like submission or compliance, but I suspect she was right thinking it something else as well. Groveling comes closer, a deeper level of shame and formlessness. She becomes a kind of spinelessness meant to be unthreatening but that is cloying and makes one cringe. In popular culture, the phrase "sucking up" has caught on, making nice to win someone in a power position, flattering to gain favor. In Annette's case, to gain a favorable look or word, to secure an attachment. At what point does this kind of subservience begin to feel like love? Where does the missing fury go?

Subservience is not a very good word to convey this process, although to serve under, to place oneself beneath touches some of it. Part of it involves being arm-less, throwing weapons away. Offering no competition to the other's ascendancy. Perhaps some of the fury goes into keeping oneself below, maintaining oneself underneath. It requires discipline to keep the other up, not to topple the one depended on.

There are fans who go crazy when a star smiles at them, but Annette's therapist wanted something more, engagement that would get somewhere. She wanted therapy to take hold, not slide into nowhere. Expectations weren't met and whatever was supposed to happen didn't. We can guess she should've done this, should've done that. We can think how we might do it better. Think anything but don't assign blame. In cases like this, blame backfires. Her therapist went on with her life and threw Annette back into the hole in the ice. But Annette did not let go so easily. She did not let go at all. Did she find Ghent's article in order to begin letting go or to cement defiance? Her response to his voice suggests she is looking for something more.

Perhaps not seeing Ghent preserves the illusion that the caring recognition he describes is possible. That love is possible. That surrender opens to it.

* * *

Loss is the flagship of Annette's life. Is it just a matter of time before what remains of the illusion of love is lost too? Is that the last thing keeping her in life? And blocking life as well?

As a little girl, an only child, she lost her mother. Is the fact that Annette clings to love, some version of it, testimony to pockets of love really tasted? Moments of love as a baby, a little girl? More than moments, perhaps a loving atmosphere? It is hard not to link Annette's disappearance with her mother's.

Her father tried to fill the gap but was unable to. He had to make a living and was away a lot. A series of caretakers came and went. When a sense of attachment began, it was the beginning of the end. Bonding became a signifier of rupture. She persisted in trying to cement what bonds she could, often with feelings that later came under names like clinging-control. Clinging as defense against the break to come.

Annette's father loved her but was not very related. He had a hard time doing more than reading his paper, watching the news, trying to simulate interest in little girl things, in another's life. He just didn't have it in him but sometimes he tried. He usually fell asleep when he played with her. Disappearance has a long and intricate history, many tributaries. He died before Annette's twentieth birthday and she sought parental substitutes coming and going in hospitals, where breaking bonds before they began (because they couldn't really begin) was naturalized.

* * *

Little by little we pieced together that her mother was depressed, at least intermittently, vacantly fading in and out, not up to life. We do not know if she was hospitalized or whether she got through it by taking to bed. The more we looked, the less support the little girl, Annette, had. Moments of love, good by comparison, islands of good or less bad feeling to hold on to. Her psyche had long been in a state of semi-collapse. She used the word hole a lot. That she had holes, disappeared through holes, was filled with holes.

The locution, to be filled by holes, is curious but telling. One thing that dawned on me that felt right was that Annette tried to fill herself with loss. She was used to filling loss with loss. Disappearance was how she filled herself.

When the bleakness she survived became visible, I was dumbstruck by the presence of love islands, imaginary or real, even if the presence of any love was premised on its disappearance. What she demonstrated with the therapist she loved was love's disappearance, over and over, until her therapist could take no more. She probably did not realize what she was getting into when she encouraged Annette to be with her and, indeed, promised not to leave.

* * *

Winnicott (1992, pp. 119–129) writes of the personality breaking apart as it is begins to form. Trauma hits at the formation of personality so that beginnings are forever associated with disaster (Eigen, 1999, Chapters 9,10; 2004, Chapter 2; 2005, Chapter 3). I think this describes something of Annette's plight. It's as if there are two poles in Annette's personality, one stronger than the other: disaster and love. What she describes by shatter and disappearance is a sense of ongoing disaster. More than a sense, it is actual disaster itself. She feels shatter, pain, disappearance that goes on and on, until it becomes unbearable, and more unbearable. An amazing quality of her life is her ability to bear pain, to bear it but not digest it. It remains in raw state without let up, getting worse and worse.

At the same time, there are moments of love and longing and caring. She helps people. She feels love. She bears witness to love at the heart of therapy, even failed therapy, therapy that rejected her, therapy that caused disastrous pain. It may be more accurate to say that therapy succumbed to the pull of pain. Potentially good work got swallowed up by disaster. Yet kernels of love persist.

It's as if her personality feeds on its illness, strengthening itself by enduring. Her life is an agony of disaster in which disaster anxiety is endured at low and high volumes. It is chronic, relentless. Now I see that the pressed look of her features is her personality pressing itself against pain. A self-pressing getting through the pain. When things go past a certain point she calls and calls and calls. I feel deep down she is looking for a mother to support her through, to the point where pain subsides and life is better. But reality is not set up for this to happen.

There is no surrender here. There is only disaster. But there are other moments, times disaster subsides closer to the background. I suspect for most of us most of the time, muted disaster anxiety is part of the background of our beings, a kind of radioactive noise in the psychic universe (Eigen, 1996, Chapter 16). For Annette it is always foreground, variable in intensity and degree. It may subside, but it is threatening, ever on the edge of becoming consuming, till what is left is hole, depression, pain, shatter, falling apart, disappearing, with no apparent end.

The other nucleus gets lesser billing. We don't know if love, as she means it, is fantasy or real, or what kind of fantasy, what kind of real. We know only that she values it. That she places hope in it and that it fails. It fails but does not end. It may be a disappearing love, allied with lots of "bad" things (control, shatter, demand, manipulation, defensiveness, fraud), but the very fact of its existence makes other dreams possible.

Having a foot in each world underlies what I've come to call Annette's "just as" experience. It is a discourse meant to elicit pity, chagrin, empathy, concern, a kind of dramatic and tragic, "Oh shucks!" or "Damn!" or "Just missed!" or "Oh no, not again!" It goes something like this: "Just as I was beginning to feel something. Just as I was about to be a patient. Just as I was able to make use of therapy . . ." Just as the wished for, ever postponed event was – finally! – about to happen, her therapist quit, stopped, kicked her out. Just as she was starting to be a person, express herself, communicate, make use of me – I wouldn't see her for free, didn't call her back or answer emails (fast enough). *Just as* IT was about to happen, the conditions that made it possible vanished or somehow came to an abrupt halt. Once more she would have to fall through a hole, endlessly disappearing.

One foot in disaster, one in hope, the former foot much larger, but enough of the latter to feel *almost, just* – before the uneven gait trips her up. Picture going through life tripping on nearly every step. You rely on depression to cushion the fall, to slow the tempo of crashes. You lose faith that getting anywhere is possible and soon stop believing that there is anywhere to get. Wherever you land, you sit and try to recuperate and just as you begin to look around, just as you begin adjusting to living sitting on the ground, you read something that touches your soul and you realize you are still alive, animate, sensitive, caring.

* * *

"You know, you're in Ghent's[2] paper. He quotes you and what you say is beautiful. You recognize other needs besides the practical and pushy. Not just love but deep contact with self. You speak of faith, he speaks of surrender. Ghent feels they go together. You both have in common a voice that makes me hear myself.

"I may never have much faith. I may never be able to open to surrender. But the urge is there. I feel the wish is powerful and good. It gives me faith in life, even though I can't back it. Even though I'm crumbling. I don't achieve the kind of integration Ghent points to. I never will. But the pointing touches something important, something I value.

"Maybe it's not so bad I come infrequently. Maybe it makes it possible for you to keep seeing me and me to keep coming. You don't let me flood you with my pain. At the end of the day, I've got to deal with it. But you don't drop me either. Maybe coming and going fits me, about as much as you or I can handle."

I wonder if surrender/faith isn't allied with reality. We work with what the situation offers and do what we can. No contradiction between faith and realism. The form of contact Annette and I have does not fit what I might have predicted. Our in and out relationship grew organically, with its own spontaneous lines. Not simply a matter of resignation but staying open to what the situation brings. A sense of acceptance that brings tears.

Is there invisible surrender within the damage? Within very per-vasive damage? With Annette it's not simply disappearance as a defense against danger. It is twinship of disaster-disappearance that seems limitless. The kind of damage we are talking about doesn't go away. One doesn't throw off one's crutches and sing praises to the Lord. One praises the Lord in the center of our gnarled selves, hunched over crutches we can't get rid of, that won't let go of us. Perhaps we might be able to live without them if we dared or knew how to, but that's a little like saying we might be able to live without oxygen if we weren't creatures who breathed. But that does not stop intimations of ineffable surrender encompassing crutches and songs, the dogged persistence of injury, pain that shatters, that makes you press yourself tightly for decades, that makes you dance while falling down. Annette despairs of achieving what Ghent describes, but the voice she hears, isn't that a bit of the sound of surrender itself?

Notes

1. E. Ghent (1990: 112–113); M. Milner (1969, pp. 384–385); M. Eigen (1993: Chapter 14).
2. E. Ghent (1990: 109, 115–116). The articles Ghent quotes are collected in Eigen (1993: Chapters 1, 11). It is more than deep joy to find my work part of Ghent's felt reflection. The fact that we resonate in profound ways through writing, brings out the amazing importance of what authors do for each other in the course of searching, stretching, reaching, bringing to life – part of what the precious gift of culture does for us and our attempts at giving.

CHAPTER SEVEN

Alone Points

I am not an emotional sea for everyone. There are people who find me remote.

A woman I love very much says, "You were good when I first came to you. You showed feeling as long as I idealized you. Now that I'm myself, you're less *there*. I need you to share more. You helped me get better and now can't take it."

I am silent. I feel terrible. I wish I could say what I feel. I don't know what I feel. I tell her I feel terrible that I can't do better, she has surpassed me in interactive aliveness, she is ahead of me. This confession of insufficiency maddens her more. "You're copping out," Jena tells me. "You're making excuses. Come out of your shell and open up."

I'm in a state I often get in. Vague, mute intensities drifting randomly, threads and cracks without clear location. Words form: "mucoid densities in viscous fields". That is what I stare at. I can't get out of it. Silenced by trauma, unborn, gelatinous, encased. Her therapist.

Jena tries to shake me up, treat me like a person. She feels I'm negative, ungiving, something she long experienced with men. She feels my disability is motivated, masking fear and hatred or a need to be patronizing and maintain supremacy by inaccessibility. A hostile withdrawal so chronic and impacted I scarcely notice it except as a sense of suffocation pressuring me into wanting to be.

At the same time, I feel good. I listen to a quiet bell deep inside me. I am sorry Jena does not hear it. What I probably mean is that I am sorry she is not satisfied with me listening to a bell inside me. She wants more. She wants me to be with her, not just inside myself. She probably has her own bell inside. She has concerns that do not reach me. Perhaps it is true that while I am listening to my bell I am inaccessible. I do not like to think that when I am alive inside in a certain way it is difficult to reach me. My skin feels the ringing and a smile from the ring begins to ripple. I realize I look like an idiot and am startled to take in the fact that my smile is insulting to her. I spend a lot of time sitting and listening, ringing and rippling. A voice inside my head says, "I don't pay you to sit and listen to yourself when you're with me." But that is exactly what I often do.

Jena asks what I am smiling about and I try to tell her but words fail. I choke on my self. I am very sad I am not better. I hate my frozen state. She does not feel me feeling her. I simply am not enough as a person. I can not find a way to make what I feel relevant. She needs more. Jena insists I am holding back, that I am not trying hard enough.

Am I imploding? Images of black hole, vortex, quicksand . . . whatever x draws me in and makes me disappear. We do not find each other. I hammer myself into the ground and disappear. I am a chronic self-hammerer, self-pulverizer. I try to make what I can't bear in myself disappear. It grows stronger and I disappear instead. Is Jena right that there is more to me than I think? She insists on speaking to me as if I were more formed, as if I were like herself, a real person. It is as if she says over and over, "Your addiction to nothingness is a disease, an excuse." She is right that I disappear because I am afraid to be there, afraid not to hide behind a semblance of giving. "That's not fair, you do give," says a voice. "What do I give?" I ask. "A bell sound in your skin," it says.

A voice that attacks, a voice that defends. Jena does not leave me and I do not leave her even though I fit her better in the beginning. We speak of mothers who are good with babies but can't take it when defiance starts and a person grows more complicated. Is there really a time before defiance? I feel tears building, bliss. I'm an empty, happy muddle, mildly at ease. A lack in a sea of feeling, a lack in a sea of bliss. Perhaps Jena can not bear to see my lack, my scar.

A self-justifying asshole is what I am. I am quiet because I dare not say a word, no excuses, no snow jobs. Do I fancy I am protecting Jena from myself, too precious about being too little? It has taken some time, but I am beginning to catch on that my vacant inadequacy is not enough for Jena. Jena rubs my nose in who I'm not. She tells me about people in her life who really *are* there for her, unlike me. I'm glad for her. Thank God, people exist who are really there. I'm not one of them, not any longer. I feared and hoped she'd find me out, that my vacancy would not be enough for her forever. She is hard on me and I am hard on myself, rightly so. Jena once felt I was being itself, her support in being. And now I am a zero.

*   *   *

There are others who feel the same way as Jena, others whom I like less or never knew well. They come for one or two visits and leave. One person did not last a session. I'm grateful to these people because they make me feel my deficiencies. They bring me to my limits quickly, without fanfare.

When you work successfully with someone it is easy to gloss over defects and limits. There is danger of self-satisfaction, self-intoxication. You get the sense that you are dealing with your problems, especially if some of your problems become a focus of mutual work. You think you are dealing with your problems because you *are* dealing with them, which is only *partly* true. You work with portions of what can be worked with, sometimes better, sometimes worse.

*   *   *

Therapy can be a heady business. Intense feelings back and forth, praise and blame and when things go well, nearly messianic preening, balanced by relief that something disastrous didn't happen. Every session is a plane crash waiting to happen. Sometimes we never come down, sometimes we never take off.

Over the years, pictures of those who left before getting started accumulate and patterns become nearly sayable. There are people who bring me to my point of silence faster than Jena. Almost instantaneously, I fall into places where speaking is impossible.

There is a kind of demanding, needy woman, very vocal about getting needs met, who invariably shuts me up, shuts me down.

I have worked with unpleasant people, women and men, for long periods, with variable success. The subset set I'm trying to describe is one I have not done well with. I'm picturing a group of angry, needy women who always want more. I never (rarely) give enough or I give the wrong thing. I just don't get exactly what I'm supposed to give or am withholding. I can try to get off the hook because I am a man: "What is it about men that can't give?" But many of these women have been thrown out by women therapists who couldn't or wouldn't take them. I can rationalize: "Maybe a detached, unfeeling man is just what they need. Anyone else couldn't bear it." I sit through anything. They attack, demand, go after their needs, seek by attacking. I clam up. They leave. I would stay with them forever but they have the good sense to leave.

Some stay for awhile. They see something good in me and insist I give it to them. I would if I could but click off, a steel sheet across my chest. They keep banging, bloody against the metal. I try and try but there is little I can do. Closing happens by itself. Sometimes I can make myself open, but they resent my effort. If I open spontaneously it is perceived as too little, too late. Always the sense of withholding the good thing or giving begrudgingly. Even in moments when I freely open, reach out, embrace – there is something about me that is simply not enough, a pinched, contracted soul. I picture someone good enough, a fuller, warmer, perspicacious being, someone better, who can really do the work that needs to be done. I imagine – I believe it is really so – that some of the people who leave me find such a person. I am happy for them and wish I could be that person.

It is little consolation that I may be such a person for some of them, some of the time. Now and then one will stay with me twenty or thirty years, hoping that something good will happen, a bit of reparation, some real work.

* * *

One woman, Karen, has been holding psychic hands with me over thirty years. Maybe, too, sitting on my psychic lap. Not lap dancing, although that sometimes is part of it. More a lap baby. She sits on my lap and it feels good to be together. We like seeing each other even though nothing happens. What happens is: we *like* seeing each other. That has meant a lot to her and made a real difference in her life.

She tolerates my holes when I vanish out of fatigue or into something unfathomable. I am aware that there are times when a Loch

Ness monster sucks me out of myself. What mainly fatigues me is I am too difficult for myself. It is hard being with another person who needs so much and you know whatever you offer is too little. I weather Karen's anger and discover she makes do with very little from me or from anyone else. Little scraps feed her for months.

You would not believe me if I told you how many therapists Karen has been through, who have, in one or another way, treated her badly or sterilely. If you are a therapist, you probably have read some of these people, heard them talk, perhaps even been super-vised or taught by them. Why she is able to find a watering hole in me, while others like her find my vanishing act unbearable, mysti-fies me. I am glad she can stand me. It partly makes up for those who can't. But, mainly – and this is most important to me – I value our contact or lack thereof for its own sake, a good or bad in itself. In this case, a bad within a good.

Karen notices I hide in my silence. She tells me she is relieved that I hide. She hides too, spends weekends in her apartment without going out, listening to music, watching movies, following shifting lines of somatic pains. She, too, fatigues herself. I know what it is like to spend weekends watching bad TV shows, not giving or get-ting, finding ways to take time off from oneself. Even though it's been a long time since I've had to do that, she knows I know what it is like. I take time off from myself in sessions and she watches me (a bad TV show). She finds it soothing as well as sometimes infuria-ting (in contrast with those mostly infuriated who bolt). "One thing I like about coming here is you don't pressure me with your personal-ity. You don't pressure me into being a person. That lets me come out of my hole now and then and get more of a taste of me."

She talks about therapists who pretend to give her something, who interpret, goose, torture her with being her. Most were trying to help, to get her to live, to be more of herself, to move past self-suffocation, past starvation. It is difficult to live with the fact that some people need to suffocate and starve a very long time, all their lives perhaps, but given care and room, more happens as well. One wishes to make trauma and deprivation go away, get on top of it, go beyond it. But sometimes there is no choice but to live with it and live with it some more. That people can have rich lives in deserts is more than a metaphor.

*   *   *

Bernadette is somewhere between Jena and Karen. "There is always someone close who does not give enough," she says. She has this recognition. But she refuses the desert and the concept of oasis. Karen, I believe, accepts me as oasis (sometimes). Oasis is not enough for Bernadette.

The concept of oasis links with paradise, the Garden of Eden, islands of goodness in difficult seas. Bernadette is not as sea averse as Karen. She likes difficulty, obstacles, tussle. She expects negativity. For her, I am neither zero nor garden. In movies, oasis is associated with mirage. Bernadette jockeys for something real, in-between, mixed, partial.

She fights ungiving aspects of others, appreciates winning through to a fuller measure. To some extent, Bernadette classifies the world in terms of the personally generous and small in spirit. She lavishes warm praise on those who are truly there for her and turns a cold beam on deficiencies of the selfish. I know what it feels like to be the object of both her warmth and coldness. Her cold beam finds me out, seeks my lesser self, rubs my nose in my emotional stinginess (sting/stingy). She makes me confront a me I hate and am ashamed of. I am at a loss. I've worked with my stingy self all my life. I will continue working with it. I feel the righteousness of her claims.

If Karen cuts me too much slack and Jena too little, Bernadette does something different: she demands I rise to the occasion but does not punish me for failing. She keeps fighting, jiggling, penetrating, going for more. She does not let up. She strategizes, pulls back, comes from another angle, relentless, persistent but not rejecting. She bides time to give me time to regroup and get ready to come to the start line. She will not let me get away. She makes me realize (again) how far people have to go to squeeze a little emotional juice from me.

I help bring others out but can I bring myself out when it counts most? I sustain myself under certain sorts of fire and demand and need. I don't think all strong women do me in. But there is blockage I try to struggle through. It took some years to reach my blocked point with Jena. In a way, she is lucky. She had a chance to have the best of me and reach a richer, fuller place in life. Is she right that I deliberately held back and kept myself out of play in a way that became important to her, or am I right to feel she reached a limit in my personality? A blockage that crumbles a little at a time over my lifetime, too slowly for Jena. I fail, clam up, shut down. Even when I break down and can not speak I support her but my support is deficient. Her edge of growth pushes me to breakdown areas. All her life she let men off the hook and now wants more. She knows how to accommodate, make do. And now insists on moving past the place of male breakdown.

What about those who do not cut me slack from the outset, who cut loose if I'm not communicative enough fast enough? I think they tune into areas of deprivation in me and fear deprivation will mount. An instantaneous sensing of deprivation that panics them into fury. Their read-out projects a painful outcome, a too painful process, too little gain. Perhaps they wonder for moments if they can teach me how to be with them, but decide against the effort. They somehow know I will not meet their needs, that I will not, can not change enough for them. Better to cut loss by not starting. Dark, angular, biting women, for whom I am not full enough.

*   *   *

I think of my Aunt Bertha, my father's sister, angular, dark, biting. The night before her wedding, she wants me to see her bathe. I resist and she brushes past resistance. She makes me come into the bathroom with her and asks me how she looks. Was there touching or was it mostly visual? Even when I was a little older, I realized she was afraid of her husband seeing her bony body, how she'd be in bed. I was not five years old. Perhaps she also wanted to show off, to glow, to be more than not too ugly. A need for reassurance driven by sexual anxiety pushing past barriers. She felt safe enough with me, a little boy. She had seen me naked since I was born.

I tried to say nice things. She pointed to her body spots, asked how this and that looked. Did I dare say I didn't like something? I was puzzled, at a loss, just wanted to get out of the bathroom. I have been somewhat disgusted, repelled by her body type ever since, even though I've had spectacular sexual experiences with women like her.

There was bitterness in Bertha, a biting tongue, often aimed at my father, as if expecting him to make up for awful deprivation. He came to America with their father without her. She remained in the old world with their mother and watched her die. I have a photo of my father in his teens working in a clothing store, trying to look grown up. Still as a teen, he taught himself accounting and did

books for local stores, then put himself through law school. He helped Bertha but she expected more and kept a special bitterness for him. Deprivation and demand, a coupling I knew early.

The day after the bathroom scene she got married in our apartment. It is said that Descartes was turned on by cross-eyed women because of a cross-eyed maid he had in childhood. I instinctively recoil when women trigger the deprivation and demand I felt in Bertha's body. Not total recoil. I liked visiting Bertha and her husband in the Bronx. They took me places in New York City. I especially loved Horn and Hardart's, the thrill of putting in nickels and lifting up a glass cover to get food, their record player (you had to wind it manually), and tropical fish tank. Nothing like these things existed in my house. Maybe she did, after all, know something about life my father didn't.

Did these nourishing experiences have something to do with my moving to New York? Have I been living in Bertha's body most of my adult life? The layering of love and bitterness reminds me of Jena, tolerating the bad for the good. When the bad gets too bad, it breaks through the good. There is only so much one will stand before the recoil.

It was a tough time for immigrants. People did not spend much time working on negative character traits. Most got used to tolerating lack and bitterness for fear of losing a chance at something good. Jena and I shared this substratum but she began to lose patience and wanted more.

* * *

A mixture of instinctive recoil, desire for nourishment, incest fear, a taste of something more – all in place waiting for women in my consulting room. Not only women. A man comes to see me or almost comes to see me. He misses his first two appointments and comes to his third fifteen minutes late. "I've not spoken to anyone for a year," he begins. "I work in my room. I don't meet anyone. I make my living on my computer. I want to talk to people. I want contact."

He speaks non-stop the remaining time, giving thumbnail sketches of his life, his pains, his virtues, his disabilities. The next day he sends an email saying he decided not to see me. He likes reading me more than speaking with me. I don't talk enough for him, whereas my books are filled with words. If he is going to reach people, he needs more from me.

It's true he didn't give me much of a chance. But while he went on talking I felt something in me shut down, not unlike what I've described above with certain women. I searched for something to say and came up empty, save for mute empathy for the pain of his life. Mute empathy was not enough. I felt myself striking out but could not do anything about it. I can excuse myself, rationalize. I fell into the vortex he lived, unable to get out of myself, unable to reach the other. Except I was reached in some fashion. I felt him, felt for him. The involution of his life moved me. Perhaps he was afraid I would smother him. I would encapsulate him inside myself. He would vanish in his pain inside me.

Maybe I simply took cover waiting for the barrage to be over. The non-stop stream of his words, pent up feelings waiting for an ear. Except feelings were largely missing. Words took their place. And I was left with wordless feelings. I felt I could help him if only he'd give me time. I also felt I could not help him. Who should I believe? Me or me? The feel of this quandary signals that I am in the domain of deprivation and demand, angry need, running from life, a desert island in a busy city. Busy minds, busy streets. I am put out of play.

*   *   *

Another man in a first session suddenly said, "Your chair is disgusting". He never came again. Someone gave me a giant leather chair years ago and it was slanted, off kilter, rundown. The sight of the chair froze the patient, drowned his words. A disgusting chair. For years, I sensed it was disgusting but never thematized it. Disgust was in the margins. As I look back on the session, I don't think he spoke a charitable word.

I imagine the chair oozing stuffing, covering the patient and myself. A token of self-disgust, mine on the surface, his disowned. My chair pushed a button. My insides took too much space in the room, covered the furniture. He could finger-point, hide his self-disgust in mine, look good at my expense. I made it easy for him.

It took me a few more years to get a new chair. But new furniture will not make what is off kilter go away.

*   *   *

I may need a certain amount of disgust, partly Bertha's heritage, other reasons as well. Maybe disgust helps me stay in contact, keeps the brakes on.

One woman, whom I felt I could help, left abruptly after a few sessions, telling me to call her if I got my office painted. My office reminded her of her psychotic mother. Being in my office was like being inside her mother. She could not bear to have therapy inside her mother's madness.

Many damaged people feel comfortable in my office. They feel a sense of relief that it is not a fancy place. Fear of being contaminated by bad stuff, madness, disgust, deprivation was too much for the woman I just mentioned. I only clicked off partly with her and hoped she could bear it.

I met her on the street years later and learned our meetings helped her more than I could have imagined. I was amazed to hear her say that meeting her mother in my office (as my office) created an opening in the madness that bound her for so long. After expressing disgust and dread of contamination so intensely, something lifted. A kind of numb, anxious paralysis gave way and she went on with her life. She thanked and hugged me. I told her my office was painted and we laughed.

*   *   *

Clamming up can come at anytime. Finding reasons only goes so far. Closing happens, stuck points. Sometimes I feel I am my stuck point, other times there is more distance. Circumstances can bring it out suddenly, unexpectedly. It hangs around waiting to happen. You will never be free of it. If you stay with it, and stay with it some more, your relationship to it may deepen. Your connection to it may become more interesting. You can't get rid of it, but battering against it, sticking your head in, looking around, dipping – something happens to you.

*   *   *

A husband and wife come for help, the wife complaining her husband is not communicative. He shuts down when she attacks him. She is not aware of being cutting. She feels she is trying to have a give and take. He can't take her contributions. She tells him, "You want me to agree with you. You feel pained when what I say doesn't fit your feeling. You have a range I'm supposed to stay within."

He has a narrow band of feeling she must conform to. I feel the truth of this in sessions, as I have little affective breathing room. He gets stiff and rigid as she chirps and chatters and I feel myself stiffening, diminishing as he defends his narrow turf. One thing that is crucial in this tenacious pattern is that what feels narrow to others seems boundless to him.

After a movie he has a deep, inchoate feeling. He is inarticulately moved and wants to remain in mute boundlessness and savor the movie's aftermath. His wife talks about the meaning of the movie. She articulates her feelings about patterns, scenes. It is as if she lobbies for its reality to her, promotes her realities. He is jarred, wishes she were silent. Maybe he wants her to align with the wordless meaning absorbing him. He is taken by wordless divinity she sticks pins into. He tries to hide from her words, lashes out himself, feels wronged, stranded, drops into mute, punishing chasms. States like this used to last for hours, days, weeks. He justified his morass by saying she carried grudges for years and he probably was right.

When they leave my office I think, "Uh-oh, here goes a wicked night, another horrible fight". The next time they say they went home and made love. Something gave, at least for the moment. The period of repair and recovery was quicker, fuller. Staying with the stuck point paid off, but who knows ahead of time when it will. Often one feels bruised, distracts oneself, does something else, Even so, intermittent staying with it shifts quality of being.

*   *   *

What feels boundless to one person can suffocate another. In the case of my male patient immediately above, his boundless movie feeling acted like a noose for his wife's self-expression. Discrepancies between inner and outer can be disastrous. An expanding person or society exerts contracting pressures.

Holding back, stifling oneself, is like not breathing. Expansion is part of life's fecundity. Shakespeare shows a point where expansion/contraction strangle each other, a tormented point. A breaking point. We are called upon to hold this breaking point without breaking, partly breaking and reshaping. We are not very good at it. It is an evolutionary call we are not permitted to give up on for very long. A pressure to stretch to make room for self and other.

*   *   *

Can patients make room for my silent spot? *Ought* they?

Jena has reached a point where tolerance of my silent place feels deleterious to her. She is ready for better. Ought she limp along with a therapist with a defect like mine? Is she ready to find someone who can be with her more fully now? She is furious with my incapacity because she does not believe I need to give in to it. I ought not succumb to self-strangulation. She refuses to. She moves through it. Why can't I? She can't believe I won't risk more, refuses to believe I can't. What is wrong with me that I can't rise to meet her growth?

* * *

Do I ask my patients to do what I can't? We egg each other on over cliff edges, taking turns refusing to make do. A profound compulsion drives us to do what we can, then more.

Not everyone is into this kind of edgy growth. One woman says being with her grandchildren is enough for her. Nothing makes her happier. She doesn't need more. Who needs psychic torture? The tormented path many seek is foreign to this woman, one of the warm of heart for whom the human is within reach. Why does she call me? Scratch a little and I learn she has a biting tongue. She is on medication, her children are. "Whatever gets you through," she says. Where does her torment go? Why does she call me? To supplement her medication? To get her through? Something more?

* * *

My silent place, paralysis, blankness, where torment vanishes. It makes sense to those who need it, a refuge at first, a spur as time goes on. A spur one can't remove, a permanent sore, irritant, push.

The man who feels impalpable depths after a movie. His wife's words are irritants. He needs his precious, private, deep feeling *and* his wife. It is important that neither go away. In this case, he seeks his irritant from the outside, another person. He escapes noticing how irritating he is to himself. It is something he must grow into. Rage and withdrawal stop him from growing into, spreading through himself.

My stupid blankness matches his resonant boundlessness. An unconscious link is made that enables him to perceive what is obvious: that his wife's words grow out of her emotional perceptions, linking depth with surface. Her words splash like stones causing ripples in waters he does not want disturbed. Does he want to be frozen like me? Disturbance mediates messages from another human being, emotional self to emotional self, much of it unconscious. Our deep permeability eludes us, enriches us. Internal states keep changing. We touch through wavering contacts, learn about emotional interchange like a baby learning to walk.

My patients sense my strangulated blankness. We learn to walk together. Sometimes they go too fast and when they fade from sight I think, "So many places I'll never get to."

* * *

Sometimes signal systems help. Signaling the other to slow down, speed up, this way, that way. Like my movie man. He learns more signals, broadens his emotional repertoire. After the movies he signals his partner, "I need time before speaking . . . wait". There are moments of special sensitivity when one needs to stop moving. People develop emotional body English, akin to learning each other's sexual vocabulary, although the latter gets more publicity.

Sometimes one prefers lack of attunement, not waiting, akin to rushing into oncoming waves, seeking exhilarating impact, the excitement of getting shook up. As when my movie man braves the first impact of his wife's words, gets tossed by turmoil, finds himself elsewhere, in another emotional setting, changed by another's words. Words, of course, do not only convey information. They mediate subject-to-subject contact, interchange, mix-up. Intersubjectivity cocktails. Being altered by each other's psyches. Words are ways of diving into each other over and over again.

Sometimes my movie man's wife is too jarring. Why can't she wait? Can't she sense him? He withdraws, sleeps on it. Emotional communication develops like invisible writing. They will never exactly get used to each other. But they have more of a sense that a lot goes on. A place opens for invisible writing.

* * *

He says, "She is insensitive to my sensitive spot."

She says, "He's a sensitivity tyrant."

She wants freer give and take. He wants fuller experiencing.

Both need time to learn more about reshuffling the deck.

* * *

Becoming one flesh (Saint Paul), a "oneness" field of emotional interchange, means mutual impact is powerful. A sensitivity bond, emotional twinship all humanity shares. Affective attitudes are interpermeable. What affects any, affects all. A wish? Ethical imperative?

The private emotional state triggered by the movie is precious. Impalpable awareness emotionally charged. Very private, yet something like it arises in a room of meditators or in shared prayer. Wordless, virginal affirmation, generic sensing, awaiting. Slowly moving towards tears of joy sensing sorrow. Quiet awe in face of emotional life. A moment of unrelatedness in which only emotion counts, as if there exists in the background of the psyche an emotional teat one sucks on, an emotional tear one hovers around like a flame. Limitlessness we can't get enough of.

* * *

Boundless silence can be a heavenly expanse where we feel that One is enough. It can contract into a ball, a vanishing point, or a womb.

A patient breaks her silence, "All one alone . . . sounds like om . . . All-one alone . . ."

Another lectures, "You worship unknown emotional force. I read your writings on Bion. Generic emotional depth transferred to ideology means war. Emotion co-opted by ideology equals death. Murder proves oneness doesn't work. We are all struggling to assert our version of reality over others."

Deep down I think, "I believe in lack of definition".

* * *

Why can't I speak? I am stuck in amorphous promise. Unformed potential means a lot to me. We are permanently neonatal, embryonic. I admire our plasticity, adaptability, our ability to draw on untapped resources when needed.

There are dangers. When my movie man is in it, other people become burdensome. One loses the richness of others. On the other hand, losing contact with the ineffable underpinning is another form of impoverishment. Can one be in two places at once? Can one ever be otherwise? An ineffable background and horizon sets the stage for living.

* * *

A note on purity. All alone with pure emotion. Only death is pure enough. Life pummels. Pure state melds with fundamentalist vision: life becomes an enemy. Life corrupts. It is too variable, unpredictable. One can't keep up with the mess or straighten it. We are into geometric buildings and design as an attempt to keep things straight, keep life tidy.

It is soothing to go to work the same days every week, do the same job with the same people. I like my routine. I grow in it. There is enough variability to keep me happy, enough continuity to keep me sane. My office, whatever its problems (too cold, too hot, too bare, too stuffed, too comfortable, too uncomfortable . . .) is cosy. It is my cave, my womb day after day, week after week, year after year. I prosper in it. Driving to it, being in it, leaving it and returning the next morning, a happiness of routine. Some find this boring. I find it a relief.

Are all human beings precious? What happens to you if you really think so?

Do you really think you can get away with the sameness of otherness? You keep your office more or less the same, a kind of self-soothing, a calculated negligence, a kind of *pars pro toto*, providing illusion of survival, a safe enough place to go on shaking.

* * *

A note on aloneness. My patient in the movie, its aftermath, emotive depths reverberating, profoundly undefined. Life vibrating meaningfully with no specific meanings, alone in the alone. People all around, partner breathing, position shifts, affect gasps, occasional whispers, annoying guffaws. What on earth do people find to laugh about! This movie cuts the bone. A room of dark presences in the womb, privacy without privacy. Complementary presences set off the jewel of self. We begin as an underwater space man in womb movies. Once out, we look to each other for forms of excitement. A relief to be out, a relief to be in. Dangerous to be out, dangerous to be in. We look to each other for a sign of life, a sign of self, a silent spot in expressiveness. Our silent aloneness needs a lot of emotional support.

* * *

None of this solves my problem with Jena. I batter myself on inner barriers. She says I do not tell her my emotional truth. I am not available. She does not feel me tear at my insides. She does not care what is happening out of sight.

I think of individuals who tell me they are unrelated or have unrelated sectors. They may be involved with partners, children, work, causes. They love. But when loss comes, they are not much shaken by it. And if they are shaken, something remains isolated, cold. They raise the question: is there always something outside the shakenness? For everyone? They feel keenly they are not like others. Others are warmer, human. They are only partly human, human to a degree, to a point. Then the cold thing takes over. Some learn about the eternal observer, witness, transcendent function. One good soul was a devote of the *Diamond Sutra*, hard cut jewel of consciousness. Another passionately asks, declares, "Can one ever undo detachment? And why *should* one?"

Coldness may soothe some, a calm in the storm, beyond perturb-ation. For others it is an irritant, a sign they are less than fully human, cold-hearted, reptilian, monstrous. I think therapy helps cushion both caring and uncaring in a semi-caring way. A place where monsters can be at home.

Silent in my alone point, unable to speak with truth, with mean-ing, chilled by trauma, immersed in embryonic potential, height-ened blankness very busy with waiting. Some patients connect with alone points of their own and others take one look and run.

None of this matters with Jena. My autistic shell, nucleus, enclave. For her it's like squeezing feeling from a stone. Sometimes I manage a few drops but the supply dries up and she feels stranded. States like this in parents make children pull their hair.

I get desperate, aloneness doesn't stop. If I sense a hidden spring within, it does nothing for her. For me the spring is not worthless. It lets me be with her in her fury, hear the rightness of her words. It enables me to outlast the storm, but outlasting does not satisfy her. I wish I could meet her in ways she wants to be met. My sense of life does not reach her. It is alone at my stuck point, stifled. My life misses hers. A hidden spring in my stuck point gives me patience, but she wants my desire, my desire's truth, honest exchange. Aloneness provides respect, a protective peace. But it is not enough.

CHAPTER EIGHT

Filling Up with Rage

"Maybe anger works better, bites off little bits of rage," says Don. He is a rage addict trying to modulate his rage. He has hit on the idea of turning rage into anger. He has a vision of rage as amorphous material, fiery silly putty, with anger a tiny bucket drawn from a great rage reservoir. Perhaps anger can leech rage and channel it.

Sounds good, makes sense. I don't buy it. Maybe some day, some way. Now it sounds like evasion, postponement, a wish. I'm sympathetic to wishes. It means Don is not happy with the way he is. He wants to be better. A wish can set a direction, propel one towards a goal. By itself it is helpless, even cruel, masking a great distance between who one is and who one would like to be, and lack of power to get from here to there.

Don makes a case for anger. "Anger reshapes rage, bends it into something workable. Rage is all-consuming. Anger leaves room in the margins."

"I worry you are slipping rage in the back door, disguising it as anger," I say, feeling guilty for not seeing progress in moving from rage to anger. Experience with rage addiction teaches me to wait and see. Rage is cunning. It finds ways to justify itself, often with twisted, hair-raising accuracy. It gravitates to faults in others and the structure of things, leeches on to other emotions, finds ways of being right, then fires. Anger can be a Trojan horse for rage.

It may sound odd to associate rage with cunning or calculation. How can something so spontaneous, overwhelming, consuming be calculated? Yet it is not unusual for elements of calculation to fuse with reactive spontaneity. Political life is filled with ways that calculated self-interest organizes rage. We seek to turn emotional life to our advantage, although our attempts often backfire.

When we rage, we look out of the corner of our eye to see our effect on others. Is the other giving in, caring, changing, bending? Rage aims to make the other penitent. There is an ought, an imperative in rage. The other should be sorry for resisting or injuring us. The other should want to make amends, mold to our will and needs. At times, we are satisfied to see the other frightened by our show of might. More often, we want the other to redress imaginary or perceived injustice.

After my Trojan horse remark, Don confesses a fear. "If I give up rage, I'll be vulnerable and alone." I believe his fear real, his thinking a bit unreal. What does it mean to give up rage? To give up any feeling? *Can* one give up rage? It sounds too ideal, too total. If he thinks he *can* give up rage, he'll persecute himself for not being able to. Like the alcoholic who swears this is his last binge, stays dry awhile, binges again. One gets mileage on both ends, rage and persecution; a double dose of intensity to fill oneself.

"Rage orgasms," he goes on. "You don't want to give up orgasms. You can't stop. You have to finish."

A kind of therapy language, to give up a feeling. Faulty locution. It's part of the way Don structures his predicament, seeing change as giving up. To surrender something negative to make room for something positive, to let go of disabling attachment. I can't help feeling this leaves him pedaling in the same spot.

He talks to himself as he talks to me, to me as he talks to himself. He sees his rage orgasm, notes its course, views it more as release than pleasure but the difference is not clear. His tone is somewhat self-disparaging, as if he is the butt of a private joke. "I'd rather have sex than rage," he says. If true, not everyone can say that.

There's not much sex in his marriage, not much of anything except fighting. Some people fight as part of foreplay. In Don's case, fighting is a deterioration of what once promised more. He is enraged that marriage gives so little. Children, yes. Relationship, no. Nothing has been as lonely as his marriage. Rage is part of his refusal to be alone.

"Part of me says, 'Go ahead, yell at her. It won't change a thing. You've lost your temper a thousand times.' " "Part" of me, this part, that part. Pieces of a me-pie? Where are these parts? Words tick off in the head, a brain-mind speaking like a bad parent, an uncaring world, "Rage, little boy. Mommy doesn't hear you."

"My wife is wrapped in defensive obliviousness," says Don. "She's perfected the art of not hearing me."

Fury falling off the end of the universe. His wife stopped listening long ago. It drives him mad, makes him want to beat her into responsiveness. "I smash. There's nothing there. My hand passes through her. A death blow does nothing. The impotence of rage." This is what he sees in his mind's eye. Beating and beating nothing. Smashing solves nothing. He rages, too, about financial debt, how impossible it is to keep up with things. She spends when there is nothing to spend. His money, like rage, gets used up with no result.

Don wants her to feel pain, *his* pain, the pain of living, the pain of *their* life together. He wants her to feel how hard it is. She seems to be oblivious. She seems to care only how hard it is for *her*. She somehow feels it's *his* fault life is hard. She does not seem to own how hard it is for *both* of them. Financial rage. Marriage rage.

"What's wrong with her that she can't feel the pain of our life together? That she can't feel how painful it is for *me* as well as her? I know it's bad for her but she doesn't know it's bad for *me*. I scream. She says, 'I can't hear you. Are you saying something?' In my mind I hear her saying, 'Ho-hum, la-ti-da'. Should I stop fighting? Should I give up? You try to build a life but there is no life. I must not be going about it the right way. But there is no right way. What do you do, laugh life off?"

Am I like his unhearing wife, my responses ineffectual? My hearing him does no good, doesn't change his predicament. Perhaps therapy, like his marriage, does not really work. Or perhaps it works a little, not enough.

There is a pause in his furious chagrin. I think he may weep. It is very quiet. After a while Don says, "Delight comes from inside". In deep meditation there is joy underneath the covers of life, under the bushes. Climbing towards the surface are complaints. If you drop down far enough, there is quiet. "Delight is large, I'm small," he says in a searching quiver. The quiet of this room is not something he has much of in his house. He can taste quivers in the quiet. Wonder, comfort, fear. He moves to the surface and speaks of the delight of sound and taste, music and good deeds, jobs well done. He reassures himself that the world outside is delightful too. Not all delight comes from inside. Where does inside come from? He needs outside anchors. Small bits of unfathomable reality to make his own.

"Big world, little me," he says. "Rage puts you in the middle of things, you connect with the center. Rage is a God connection. You feel bigger when you rage. You feel like God when you rage. Maybe God, too, feels bigger when He rages." Rage comes because Don is afraid to settle. He gives in to rage to escape giving in to life.

Don speaks of King Lear's rages, a tragedy of vanity, love's destructiveness. Rage fading into blackness. Don and his wife loved each other once. Delusion? Attraction, the power of youth? Ignorant of what time exacts, the work of living together? He cries, "How small we are. Why God? You make us like ants. Rage obliterates our ant-ness. After rage, ants come out again. Rage can't keep up with them. You can't stop it, can't get away – you need your ant-ness." Our ant-ness, not God's. Don switches abruptly from God to self, speaking to himself, to me, the "you" of humanity.

"If you see it, you live differently. Lear didn't see it until it was too late. He felt powerful and lost his power. Therapists speak about giving away your power. I had a dream with words something like this:

Ants devour ants.
We're not just ants.
We're radiant beings.

"Lear traps me. Radiance frees me. Whoa: rage can be radiant too. Radiant rage. Maybe there's no way out. No way out or in. How important do I have to be is the question? The more important, the more impotent. A radiant ant, that's a possibility I may have over-looked. A radiant ant together with other radiant ants." Don is weepy. The feel of life touches him. It is not that conflict stops, it's that, for the moment, the fact that he is so steeped in conflict touches him. An immovable tragic element moves him, a sense of poignancy about the radiant agon of ants.

Don cracks his head against his wife, his life, his rage, his fury. Something shifts, tastes different. A taste he can't pin down makes him wonder.

* * *

"My rage is draining," says Melissa. "Is anything else there?" She feels defeated by rage, deflated. She jumps up, rushes to the bathroom to see herself in the mirror. She looks fine. She's there. Not at all as she pictured. Three dimensional outside, inside fading.

"I need my rage. I can't teach without it. Kids go haywire. They'd be all over the place if my rage didn't get their attention, hold them together." Melissa depends on rage to organize the classroom, to make her presence felt. Rage conveys demand. It spills over to her family, parents, husband, children. Her home, like her classroom, is a nest for rage. Rage is part of her will to be sincere, part of a fight to be true to what things mean to her. It breaks out, haywire, when the latter is challenged.

"A sad deflated ball covered up by warrior rage. I have a student who has greatness of spirit. Rage is part of it. But the other day she was sad, shrunken. I held her hand. My heart went out to her but I was afraid and recoiled, fearing my touch a death grip. I would hold her and never let go. She would become part of me. I did not want to drench her. I want to support her, let her swim, fly. I'm a walking trap. I want to never let go, so I push away. But I reached her, touched her through my fear.

"I know some teachers put kids in boxes. They're afraid of getting touched. What can they do for these kids? You can't survive emotionally if you don't hold back. You look at the kids and see so many wrenching stories, so many in need of help. You've got to keep your distance. You can only do what you can do. The girl my heart went out to: I could choose to keep her in a tiny spot inside me, a little tidal pool, or let her into a broader area. Her pressing into me enables me to feel more of me, a broader area, as if she is creating an area in me for her and waits to see how much of it I can offer. I can be smaller, larger. All this in a few instants. You choose what kind of person you are going to be, more or less.

"I feel better speaking like this. I feel the kids more when I'm not yelling. They enter more fully into the mainstream of my psychic life. When I yell, I feel OK I have to do this, I have to get the job done. But something in me doesn't buy into it. I used to think, that's the real me, the yeller. Now I feel there's more of me in calmer moments. When I speak like this feelings have a chance to circulate.

"When I touched her hand, I touched a soft center. She's like a preemy and I'm an incubator keeping her warm and helping her breathe. She warms me too. We're both so sensitive. I knew I could not go all the way. I was already pulling back, afraid of myself, thinking I'm an octopus. Or a shark. Do you know an octopus can kill sharks? I fear my octopus will suffocate sharpness. We're both transfusing each other with teeth, with softness."

Melissa condemns herself for not being sensitive enough, for being too sensitive or sensitive the wrong way, for being a killer shark, a suffocating octopus. She never gets it right yet swerves from the full force of self-hate. She knows we are engaged in some kind of emotional transfusion.

"I need to be a shark to survive but am ashamed of how much of a shark I become," Melissa says plaintively. "When I was young, my mother called me Attila the Hun. When I was a teen, my rage had a smearing, sneering quality. In college I was smart enough to package it. I could play with it, tone it down, so I usually got away with it. Some people thought I was smug. Smugness is quiet rage, quieting yourself by tightening. I have an advantage over my student. She has less access to her cruelty. She gets bruised and battered and covers up a lot. She responds to a soft touch." Melissa and I are quiet for a long time. I feel weepy. We listen to each other breathing.

"I seem to wait to get here to take a deep breath," she says.

* * *

A few sessions later, we're at square one. Melissa tells of raging at one of her children. "It came from a black point, a tornado, through a demon in my mouth. I could scream until the scream dies out. It dies out where no bones or flesh are left. Screams crumble, turn to dust. You scream the pigment out of you." She means you scream until life's coloring vanishes.

"It's more flooding than paralysis," Melissa says. "Paralysis is covered by concrete. The scream comes from a place where I have to share skin. My mother wants us to have the same skin. My scream disintegrates. It does not get her out of my body. It fades. It scares people outside. But anyone inside doesn't care. My mother doesn't hear it." Her mother doesn't but her child does. She terrifies her child, draws emotional blood, feels a full impact on someone, an annihilative impact. Far from helping, it makes things worse.

"I'm reduced to tearing my skin. Maybe I can cut her out of me. It's not just her I'm trying to get out. It's something essential, the way life feels. No one can cut it out. You can't turn it into a tumor and be done with it. Doctors cut body parts out for people. What are they trying to remove? I want to rub my skin with sandpaper and exfoliate confusion. I want to clear my skin so I can have a proper cover."

Melissa expresses a wish to be new, wash foreign matter away, clean mater's sickly influence, end malignancy. She has inklings this is impossible. She would have to cut life out to make mother go away, She would have to wipe out the wiping out tendency. "You can't get rid of all the dirt that clings to you," she says. "I clean my house, my skin, my clothes, my thoughts. I can't stop things from coming inside me, from welling up." Even if her mother could be excised, life would still threaten her with living.

I dream of fucking Melissa. Actually, we're not fucking but thinking about it. I touch her tit and she gets hot. Another woman is in the bed. Won't it end therapy? We hope we can do it and continue therapy. The sex feeling is so strong it feels like we did it, although we were still talking about it.

When we next meet, Melissa says she wants my rage. Not just my mind, my intuition, my interest. She wants my rage to fill her. She wants my worst, something ugly. She wants our relationship to be real.

To be filled with breath, with food, with sex, with feeling.

* * *

Brennan holds his belly, rolls on the couch, picks up his legs, thighs to chest, breathes rapidly, stifles a howl. What I hear sounds like a wounded animal, except it is a person's soul stricken nearly silent with grief and rage. He is trying to *say* something about what he feels, let what he feels *speak*, find expression. His twitches and moans are perfectly communicative but he wants more.

He speaks of intense desire for his mother with no possibility of gratification. Something he learned in therapy? Opening to the impossible? He is searching for the real, no room for anything less.

Mother language is meant to express failure. It is not just wanting mother. It is fidelity to something gone wrong, something essential.

"Her contact with me was impaired," Brennan says. His desire for her was more than sexual. Brennan's life formed around an impaired core. An invitation from a woman who was not there. Delicious skin, now and then a radiant face. Promising eyes that proved pointless. In the middle of touch, she disappeared. Self to self contact was missing.

An efflorescence of psychopathic indulgence grew up around the no-contact core of Brennan's family. He depicts his mother as a beauty absorbed with promoting herself. She wanted him to think she was a feast, but was impatient to get away. For his father, contact meant winning someone over, getting what he wanted. He elicited admiration to cover flaws. Brennan felt caught between parents who acted somewhat like parents but could not come through. Both wanted to be appreciated for being what they could not be. Brennan felt pressured to play along, pretend they were great, but was in hell. He soothed himself with success from childhood on, but hell mounted. By the time he saw me, he pretty much realized hell would never go away.

He lived a successful life around a no-contact core. One thing he learned from his parents: all the tricks to get admired. He was impacted in layers of personality dedicated to winning admiration. A difference from his parents was his determination to come through, as a parent, as a person. He did not want to foist himself on others as an illusion. His knowledge that he dissimulated for admiration tortured him. If he failed to be a person, this failure, unlike his parents, agonized him. His need for an honest life, a life of real emotional nourishment, far from making him satisfied, fuelled self-hate. He could not forgive himself for being so far from what he wanted to be. Inside this hate, too, was the inability to forgive his parents for being what they were. Inside this hate, a lot of hurt.

Brennan tells me about a friend speaking to him about cutting himself and others slack. He can't stand slack, needs taut. Pull the strings of self tight, don't let anything get away – don't let himself get away with anything. "You're too harsh with yourself, too hard on everyone," says his friend. Hard-on is a buzz word for Brennan. He needs his body to be hard, no fat, no softness. He is threatened by softness. His wife's face and body are hard. He complains about her toughness, but needs it. His friend advocates compassion. A little like telling a color blind person to see red.

Brennan knows compassion is a missing nutrient. "The world is filled with hard-ons," he says. "Can you stand entertainers on talk shows babbling like babies? People with money admired for money? People with power admired for power? Is that what it's about? Can that be IT? *They* believe they deserve good things. *They* give themselves good things with a vengeance, forgive themselves anything. Is that what you mean by forgiveness? What about struggling with goodness?

"My parents were the celebrities, the powers of my childhood. They refused pain. I am the pain they refused. They escaped struggle with themselves but didn't escape misery. Pain doesn't vanish because you pretend it does. I bear the pain they refused. They hid their fear of going under and I'm stuck in it.

"Didn't it hurt to see their child burn with the suffering they avoided? 'You're too sensitive!' my father would say. 'You make everything a big deal. Toughen up, like I did.'

I pretend to the outside world but inside is horror. Raw nerves, holes to hide my rage in, hurt choking on rage. It's frightening to think inside ourselves is the horror the world lives out. Isn't that what Job is about, horror inside righteousness?"

Brennan lies quietly as the current subsides. We wait for the next wave.

He confides, "The world I lived in was worse than growing up with parents who couldn't be parents because of physical disease. I lived with psychic disease. No place to touch reality that wasn't dreadful. Moments of beauty and truth made the horror clearer. Now I'm a creature crawling in your office, a figment of the unbearable."

Brennan is amazed people can't see every word they say, every gesture they make are parts of an invisible explosion. He feels his belly churning, burning and turns to his immediate life, his wife. "She carries the spore and antidote. A critical eye, a loving heart. A heart dying to find another caring core. A merciless eye boring in, up and down my backbone. An eye that leaves no room. She doesn't show this eye outside the family. She saves it for us. Her criticisms make the kids shudder and leave me nowhere to go. No place to say, "OK. I'm not *that* bad – I made a mistake." She pins me to my narcissism, pushes hard into me. She doesn't see me falling. I desperately try to attach myself to my narcissism with rods, wires, sticky stuff, while I slide into nothing.

"I wonder what would happen to you if you lived outside of human connection, making others want to connect with you, and when they reach out they find a murderous psychopath but may never know it. It's real to keep me at arm's length. I look inside and see a father and mother locked in malevolent embrace. They'll cut you to pieces if you show signs of caring.

"My wife cares. I know it. I'm afraid of what I'll do with it. A wary belief is growing: I believe she really wants to talk to me."

His wife pins him with her eyes, seeks him with her heart. There is no space inside her eyes but there is space in her heart. The fact that both are real forces Brennan to stretch.

"I'm ashamed of my feelings. They're undeveloped, vain, infantile. This is a confession. I feel sentimental things, gushy things at movies. What moves me? Reunions. Or a judge on court TV saying, 'You two should be together.' I look like someone who survived the end of the earth. At the end of the earth there is a sun in my heart, breaking it. Some people like the broken look, but not many want to have it."

*   *   *

"Something unreal clings to life. I've felt this ever since I can remember," says Kirk, who could not speak for a long time and now can't stop. "It does not have to be painful. It can be dreamy, floaty. It is horrible when you can't shake it, when you're in the middle of something real, something that means a lot to you. You're with your children and the unreal spreads. It stains the time you are together.

"It often keeps its place, an accompaniment, an undertone, a film. Life goes on, solidly, fully enough. The real, the unreal make a deal. They get along. Then something happens that throws the balance off and they fight for territory. You'd think it fine for the real to win, but the real can take more than its own and create danger. The unreal fights back, spreads through life's openings, stains surfaces. It is unsafe, unwanted and doesn't care.

"I've tried everything. Body therapies, medication. I'm tired of the latest thing. Eye movement, foot massage, head massage. Why are there so many therapies? Is it that every part of us cries for attention? The last psychiatrist I saw told me the unreal was in my brain and imaging might locate it. He could zero in on it with medication. The hope that medication could make unreality go away or lessen it – I know it works for others, but something weird happened with me.

The unreal feeling thinned, then got spotty, then layered by other unreals. I felt lighter, more alive for a time. But bothered that the unreal feeling became unreal. One unreal cancelled another. I got weirded out. It was bad enough to be unreal but now I was haunted by ghosts of the unreal. Medication made the real more real, but the unreal would have its own.

"It's a relief to sink into work with you. A scary relief. You don't seem to make demands. You're not trying to get me better. It's non-work. Maybe you don't think I can be cured. What would cure mean? Feeling only real? Less unreal? Living better with unreal and real me?

"It's hard to get used to not passing judgment on being unreal. Some therapists said the unreal was anger against myself. Rage with nowhere to go except to blow myself away, numb myself. The goal was to put my anger into words, direct it outwards, relieve the pressure of hurt feelings. I tried trauma therapy, scream therapy, to make my tissues come alive, to make my soul come alive. When the dust settled, I was me again, real me sometimes, unreal me a lot. I failed to push past myself.

"You don't seem to care. It's not that you're indifferent, although sometimes I wonder. It's more that you don't take sides. You hear both out, unreal, real. Both have a playmate. Maybe it's just that unreality doesn't freak you out. You're so unreal you don't care about it anymore. It's part of things, guests, even if they stay a life-time. I feel less odd being me when I'm with you. Maybe you're so odd I feel OK. It's a relief to feel I can be unreal and not keep tucking it in, pinching in. Reality-unreality cocktails. I feel more comfortable being me with you.

* * *

"I wish you'd talk more. I wonder if you're there. You're waiting me out. I feel a rage at waiting. When you talk I wish you were quiet. Getting things just right is not something I have to worry about. My mother bugs me even though she's dead. I dream she is alive. I should treat her with compassion. I feel fury that she haunts me in my dreams. Even in death she's controlling. She puts her deadness into me. I fear something bad will happen because I don't feel kindly to a spirit.

"Bitterness entered me in her arms. Now I'm bitter with my wife. Love makes me cranky. Love is kindling for rage. Notice: kind – one of a kind, my kind, your kind – being kind – kindles rage. I breathed my mother's breath. She wants to fill herself with me, wants me to love her. I have a defect: love infuriates me. She expects love to be more. Love is unreal. When it is real, it is pain. There is failure built into more.

"Do all infants rage at mother's failure to be more? I don't think so, not if a mother does not try to be everything, not if she is someone a baby can forgive. To be someone a baby can forgive – *that* is something worth striving for.

"My father's bitter rage was not like my mother's. I can't tell who was more rageful. He was louder. She sucked it in. He'd explode, she'd cajole. Sometimes it seesawed the other way. Rage is depressing. I'd withdraw, hide in my room, relieved to be by myself. Lonely and relieved. 'My mind to me a kingdom is.' I read it in high school. 'The world is my own.' These are things I'd think. I don't know who was most depressed. I'd stare out the window fogging out, staring into myself, a gray expanse. Bitterness fades in absorption.

*   *   *

"I wish I were someone else in my marriage. I despise the way I am with my wife. I'm corrosive, crabby, try not to give in to myself, try to act better. Crabgrass is voracious. I would have to spend all my time weeding but I don't want to live such a guarded life. If I give in to my rage, I would end up alone. My wife would leave. I feel the pull to be alone. I never realized how much rage and aloneness go together. They are a nested couple, pulling and pressuring each other, drawing me in. I should get away but I'm interested. A mysterious destructive force keeps me in life, propels me into living."

The force Kirk talks about unites with Brennan's no-contact, the latter an implosive force coming from all directions. Don, too, reacts to not being heard and goes through life emotionally tone deaf. Being emotionally tone deaf is one reason he feels safe in movies, where his hunger for feeling can be appeased without having to respond to another person. Melissa's rage also touches a need to feel filled, to fill up on feeling, in dread of lean times. All four suffer and reach out from deeply withdrawn places, where severed nerves blow up like mines when stepped on, raw spots touched by fellow sufferers.

CHAPTER NINE

Boxes of Madness

There are many threads in psychoanalysis and madness is a privileged one. Freud's structural concepts are imbued with portrayals of madness. Id as a seething cauldron of excitations, no no in the unconscious, opposites meld, reverse, are indistinguishable, the law of contradiction and common sense do not hold. Ego as hallucinatory organ, idealizing-denigrating (over-underestimating), projecting, identifying, denying, splitting, disintegrating; a double agent, developing anti-hallucinogenic properties and perceptual, reflective sanity. A sanity often soaked with madness that seeps through personal and world events. A superego concerned with morals, turning moralistic, overly self-critical, punishing, cancerously destructive, devouring reality with hate-filled ideals. Freud takes us to places where madness stains psyche. Capacities that try to set things right are not exempt. Psychoanalysis can lay no special claim on sanity but joins the struggle, replacing obsession with sin by analysis of madness, opening possibility for further ethical development (Eigen, 1986: Chapter 1).

It took time for psychoanalysis to come out of the closet and trace psychotic processes masked by neurotic organizations. "Behind every neurosis is a hidden psychosis": a remark I heard Henry Elkin make in the late 1950s, if not a rallying cry or psychoanalytic koan, expresses a current that gathered momentum. A current that fit a thread in cultural life concerned with meaninglessness, disintegration, destruction, emptiness, warp. Disaster that hit not only individual personalities, but the social fabric.

Many voices bearing witness to psychotic dynamics arose, Melanie Klein's one of the strongest. She does not say every human infant is mad, but she does say all have psychotic anxieties. Some felt anxiety too weak a word and spoke of agony (Elkin, 1972; Winnicott, 1989), catastrophe and nameless dread (Bion, 1970). Still, Klein put madness on London's psychoanalytic map and changed the direction of British psychoanalysis. Her sail caught a wind already blowing, but few went as far with it.

Her background includes Karl Abraham in Germany and Sandor Ferenczi in Hungary, rich envisioners of early states of mind. Both were concerned with the fate of destructive urges. Abraham (1973) emphasized oral sadism and Ferenczi (1955) the importance of the mother in modifying an infant's death drive. Association of psychosis and destruction was part of the air Klein breathed and she gave it significant turns.

She picked up on Freud's depiction of infantile hate in relation to externality, together with the infant's attempt to expel disturbance. In her vision (Klein, 1946), the infant tries to rid itself of disturbance by splitting it off and projecting it outwards. This assumes some good feeling nucleus that attempts to go on maintaining good feeling. One positively identifies with a good feeling current, negatively identifies with bad feeling. This is an extremely important emphasis, a movement that informs her thinking. The infant tries to rid itself of pain and disturbance without knowing the source of the irritant or how to relieve it. It gets rid of bad feeling by changing its place, displacing, hallucinating or imagining it elsewhere. It gets rid of bad feeling by placing it into an outside object.

An object outside of what? An object caused by bad feeling to begin with? Bad feeling attributed to an object, bound as an object? Her work abounds with inside objects placed outside, outside objects absorbed inside, a kind of psychic breathing. Doubleness permeates her work. Split drives, affects, ego, objects. Almost a psychic gnosticism: good and bad warring throughout the psyche.

One of the greatest war zones is the mother's body, good and bad breasts outside, good and bad babies, wombs, penises, rivals inside. The infant's psyche swims through maternal insides encountering rivals, father's penises (good and bad), golden milk babies and spoiled fecal ones, good and bad mothering moments solidifying as objects locked in strife. The confused, agonized baby god attempts to split regions of being, separate good from bad, inside from outside, triumph over rivals, control mother's insides (body, mind), access and own the greater god's creativity (to generate babies, milk, thoughts, feelings). To feel good and keep feeling good: an activity confused with winning.

The Kleinian baby is very busy controlling bad things, keeping the good going. Where is the good located? In body sensations, affect sensations, attitudes? Mixtures that keep shifting? How does one shift with it, keep up with it, as good-bad conditions change? Mother's body, an hallucinated heaven based on heavenly moments, turns out to be an arena of threat, conflict, challenge and terror as well.

Psychic breathing is more complicated than physical breathing. It is not just a matter of expelling bad, taking in good. Good and bad are inside and outside, fused and split. The Kleinian psyche is a kind of fantasy pump, circulating good and bad affects/ego elements/objects inside and out in order to keep a modicum of good feeling going in face of the ever pressing bad.

A pass Klein brings us to, of crucial importance, is use of good feelings, a part of psychic reality, to blot out, substitute for, displace bad ones. Good blots out bad with variable success, bad returning, even blotting out good for a time. Good and bad feelings in tension, struggling, magnified through the prism of fantasy. The good trying to offset the bad, the bad threatening to overwhelm the good.

An inherently stressed, pressured psyche trying to maintain good feeling in face of bad. Great tension, great struggle. A war psyche. Every capacity potentially defending against and attacking every other. A psyche constantly trying to keep up with its own destructiveness.

Death and life drives: Freud

A turn occurred in psychoanalysis, shifting emphasis from sex to death (Eigen, 1993: Chapter 9; 1996: Chapters 1–2). Freud associated anxiety with sexual excitement, which had to be modulated for the sake of individual, social and cultural development. A depressive-anxious tendency attended sexual desire as part of the latter's cultural formation. Anger was part of passional energy, as index of frustration, as force to overcome obstacles, as part of energic vigor, as part of self-affirmation, as response to threat. Social and professional injury (blows to the ego, blending injury with anger) important in themselves, tapped infantile sexuality, impossible wishes, re-routing of desire. Repressed sexuality, its symbolic spread through culture, together with an angry mix of depressive anxiety, formed a grouping that, after thirty years of intellectual and clinical labor, Freud (1920; 1940) associated with life drive, libido, a tendency to weave drives, affects, objects into more complex unities, a tendency to build.

After thirty years of labor, Freud also posited a destructive force that was more or other than the anger of the life drive. A force that worked against growth, a kind of entropy, inertia, catabolic tendency breaking down unities. As if psychic life, too much for itself, tore itself down and/or collapsed under its own weight, unable to take its own pain, its sensitivity, the challenge of its own development. To be something and suffer and grow or to be stress free nothing, i.e., not to be.

One sees this shift in the change of meaning of death wish, which earlier meant our angry wish for others to die, and now expressed a force aimed against ourselves (Freud, 1920, 1937; Eigen, 1986, 1996). Freud analogizes life and death drives to anabolic-catabolic processes, a quasi-biological substratum for psychic forces: to build up, to tear down, parallel to symbolic-diabolic, to tie together and break apart.

Some call Freud's death drive a cancer psychology, a war psychology, a death psychology growing up as it did after the First World War, the death of a daughter, his own cancer. Whatever the fate of the death drive as a scientific concept, it ripples with meaning, a portent, a warning, a signifier of ghastly things humans do to each other, to themselves. A concept burning with horror, the Holocaust incubating, its impulse very alive today.

Death and life drives: Klein

Melanie Klein's formulations are rooted in Freud's death drive: "I hold that anxiety arises from the operation of the death instinct within the organism, is felt as fear of annihilation (death) and takes the form of persecution" (Klein, 1946: 296). A destructive force in the organism translates to global annihilation dread, distilled as particular object fears. Objects may be internal or external, images, persons or parts of persons, affects, character traits, attitudes, somatic functions. Conscious or semi-conscious persecutory fears tap generic unconscious destructive currents rooted in the organism. The psycho-organism, under tremendous destructive pressure from within, filters some of the latter through objects.

One scenario is for intrinsic annihilation dread to be felt as caused by objects. We try to control annihilation anxiety by controlling objects we imagine responsible for it. One such process is to introject the object, taking in and circumscribing disturbance one hoped to expel. If only one can concentrate disturbance, packet it, export it, place it elsewhere. Like the return of the repressed, projected/introjected annihilation works partly, for a time.

A scenario we dumbly repeat is to split off and project disturbance and try to kill it off by killing objects we think cause it. In effect, we try to kill the death drive by killing objects symbolizing it. Horror escalates as attempts to annihilate signifiers of annihilation fail in unconscious aim. This is not to say we are not afraid of murderers or that murder is not real. Likewise, disease and death. This is not a stupid theory. There are many sources of anxiety. Psychoanalysis adds unconscious surplus: global, pervasive unconscious dread of destruction, rooted in the organism, magnified by unconscious fantasy, working by projection–introjection. Conscious dreads tap unconscious dreads. Klein compounds some of the latter (death and birth anxiety, separation anxiety, bodily frustration) into the term "primary anxiety", dread with many faces, at many levels of being.

We have moved from reading symbolic displacements of repressed sexuality, to symbolic traces and enactments of death-work: from sexual-aggressive anxiety to annihilation anxiety. Freud wrote that every psychic act combines death and life drives. Klein emphasizes the function of life drive as defense against death drive. The life drive works to offset the death drive, to mitigate destruction. It is as if the death drive is more basic and powerful and the life drive tones it down for a time. Life as defense against death, a postponement. One reason we feel the press of time is that life is hard pressed to keep up with death. For Klein, life drive and objects function to regulate, offset, modulate the death drive.

Splitting and projective identification

The ego splits in order to modulate the flow of death, toning death down by distributing it across affect and object fields: "The result of splitting is a dispersal of the destructive impulse which is felt as a source of danger" (1946: 297). Klein links "the primary anxiety of being annihilated by a destructive force within", and the ego's splitting or falling to pieces, with schizophrenia. Schizophrenia results from an annihilative process defending against further annihilation.

Splitting can proliferate, multiply, go on forever, the result being a fading or thinning of affect, a sense of being unreal, oscillating with hyper-real, depending on whether the diffusing or intensifying aspect of splitting dominates at a given time. While psychosis is an all too rigid, stable organization, a good deal of fluctuating extremes go on in it, the personality obsessively-hysterically shifting grounds, in a panicky, paranoid driven way within a quasi-delusional mode. Psychosis is both a result of and attempt to regulate destruction, the latter usually quite visible in the individual's concerns and fears. It is as if a person in the grips of psychosis is asking, "Will this destroy me? Will this destroy me?" – as he or she bounces from one thought or feeling or image or external danger to another. Another way of putting it: "What will I have to think or do, it order to preserve the world and myself?" Since splitting the destructive drive works through any psychic function or product and does not stop, spreading anywhere and everywhere, no safe haven can be found for long, neither out nor in. The idea that there will not be destruction is as delusional as the idea there is only destruction. We modulate, even transform destruction as we can, but there is no end to it.

In Klein, splitting acts to separate good from bad, but also goes on in the destructive domain. In the first case, splitting tries to protect good from bad, separate them, split off and project the latter. As noted earlier, good-bad may apply to affects, objects, ego states. To preserve good objects or self-states in face of inner attack is a necessary, thankless task. The psyche's work is never done. There is no end to maintaining a modicum of goodness in the midst of destructive tendencies. Islands of goodness in a sea of destruction. A bit like the sorcerer's apprentice, bailing out the psyche, a ship full of holes. To compound difficulty, the psyche tries to control destruction by splitting the destructive tendency, projecting it, diffusing it, dispersing it throughout internal-external universes. Psyche works overtime, keeping bits of goodness good, flushing out bad in ways that multiply the latter.

This sounds a bit like St. Paul's portrayal of the law. Laws multiply to preserve justice, goodness, purity – partly degenerating into superstition. Which side of the bed to get out of, which leg to put down first, which shoe to put on first become ritualized. Something destructive may result if the regulating rule or law is not followed correctly, faithfully. The magical fallacy of such rules does not mean the destructiveness they respond to is unreal. On the contrary, it shows to what extremes we are driven under destructive pressures. The Bible is a kind of handbook to regulate destruction, with more or less success in various contexts. It may send us off in wrong directions, but is filled with important hints.

Klein encapsulates her vision by postulating an early *paranoid-schizoid position*, in which psyche handles disturbance and pain by attacking it, splitting it off, projecting it. It hates disturbance and makes it go away. If hate disturbs, it hates hate, tries to make hate go away. However, it is inwardly identified with the exiled elements, since they are all parts of oneself. One is in the position of banishing parts of one's mind in order to regulate psychophysical disturbance. Thus the term, projective identification: split off aspects of the self one unconsciously identifies with, but which are projected elsewhere to minimize disturbance. The offshoot is a chronic state of re-routing annihilation anxiety via splitting and projection, while remaining unconsciously identified with exiled aspects of death threats. Outer and inner universes become peopled with projective displacements of annihilation anxiety linked to a destructive force within.

Klein points out the self-defeating nature of this primitive operation. For example, one introjects objects containing our projections, re-infecting ourselves with what we try to get rid of, compounded by the other's projective work as well. Ideally, the other will work over our projections, transform them for the better, so that what comes back is not as bad as what went out. Klein stresses that projective-introjective identifications are fantasy formations. So that distress is magnified imaginatively – a witch, rather than mother, a devil, rather than father, a pit of hell, not simply a stomach. We try to regulate destructive feelings with destructive fantasies, attempt to relocate destruction, shift it away, an operation doomed to boomerang.

Double nuclei, goodness, idealization, denial of psychic reality

Klein posits a double beginning or a doubleness in beginnings, in keeping with Freud's dual drive theory, life and death drives. The phrase, "in the beginning," appears in her work repeatedly. Over and over she says that aggression and hatred (death drive deflected outward by projection) play an important role from the beginning of life and that from the beginning the first internal good object does as well. The "first internal good object acts as a focal point of the ego. It counteracts the processes of splitting and dispersal, makes for cohesiveness and integration, and is instrumental in building up the ego" (1946: 297).

This is a momentous shift of emphasis. An internal good object, outreach of the life drive, functions not as a primary source of anxiety (sexual excitement), but to allay, mute, bind anxiety about destruction. The good object, with its sense of wholeness, functions to counteract outreaches of death-work, splitting and dispersal, themselves attempts to distribute destruction in order to survive or ease it.

States of frustration intensify the workings of the death drive, leading to attacks on breast, object, ego. If things are bad enough, destructive attacks extend to sensation, feelings, thoughts, the mind or body itself, splitting self and other into bits and pieces, worlds of hate-filled shards. Amalgams of sensation, affects, ego and object, imaginings, body elements and functions fuse and fly in different directions, threatening to pull self apart even more, issuing into bits of threatening figures everywhere, inside and outside the body. One's own destructive feelings spread through one's organs, real and imaginary, populate inner and outer horizons.

As the quote above suggests, a good object is present too, counteracting destructive divisiveness, tending towards cohesion (the unifying life drive) and development. "I hold that the introjected good breast forms a vital part of the ego, exerts from beginning a fundamental influence . . ." (1946: 295). The good object from the beginning helps mediate growth of self and object relations.

What we have, in part, is a psychoanalytic phenomenological/ visionary working out of ways life and death drive work through unconscious fantasy (projective/introjective identification), distributing through creative-destructive ego and object relations, including maturation of affective connection. The support of a good object/ego/affect nucleus from the outset is crucial, or there would be only destructiveness, i.e. nothing at all. Inherent tension between goodness and destruction seems to be basic. A variation of this is the Catholic notion that evil feeds on good, a positive for destruction to destroy. Today, I suspect we wonder if destruction needs only itself to work on.

The good breast makes one feel complete, is felt to be complete itself (p. 297). A completeness shaken by frustration, pain, anxiety. A sense of completeness makes one more secure, a necessary illusion perhaps, but one that can be dangerous. Sometimes the completion of goodness feels suffocating and one tries to break through it. One tries to break self or others apart to recover fragmentary states. At times, destruction feels more real.

We have, then, a kind of gradation. Good feelings that support the self, good feelings that suffocate it. A sense of completeness that adds cohesion and completeness that feels unreal and invites fragmentation. Klein notes that extremes of good feeling correlate with persecutory fears. Not simply that we feel persecuted by good feeling (something she does not consider fully), but that good feeling – idealization, idealized good feeling – binds or counteracts persecutory anxieties. Idealization and persecution as two sides of a split coin: exaggerated good breast or object protects against the annihilating bad breast or object. Translate this as you will, the function pointed to is important.

There are splits within splits within splits. Good-bad breasts or other objects, aspects of breasts or other objects, idealization-persecution, and so on. After delineating the good object as a pivotal nucleus at the heart of personality, necessary to support growth, she develops what I feel to be a quintessential Kleinian theme: use of goodness to deny, even obliterate, psychic reality. Exaggerated goodness, idealized goodness or an idealizing function of goodness perhaps. Or more profoundly, hallucinated goodness, partly built from good memories, perceptions, fantasies.

Klein amplifies Freud's fantasy of an infant hallucinating a good feed when hungry, substituting pleasure for pain, satisfaction for distress, a wish-fulfillment. Freud's hallucinated satisfaction slides into perfection, a beatific or ideal state. A sense of wholeness, completion, fullness when one is helplessly on the verge of dread, panicky hate, falling apart, screaming oneself to oblivion, dying. Good feeling masking persecutory anxiety, the latter a more limited profile of generic destructive force. How easily Freud threads into Klein.

Instinctual desires, aiming at unlimited gratification, "create a picture of an inexhaustible and always bountiful breast – an ideal breast." Also called, "an idealized object" and "ideal object." Splitting and hallucination work together, a hallucinatory splitting off of the good, making it all good, making goodness all (1946, p. 299). An affective sensation that finds its way into and supports the wish or belief or intimation or conviction or goal: to live forever in a state of happiness.

We reach an amazing insight: "In hallucinatory gratification, therefore, two interrelated processes take place: the omnipotent conjuring up of the ideal object and situation, and the equally omnipotent annihilation of the bad persecutory object and the painful situation" (1946: 299). Is it the life drive that is annihilating the death drive or the death drive annihilating itself? Individuals and groups attack one another, partly in hope of annihilating annihilation, only to discover pain, often horror, that hallucinatory positions fail to cover.

As Freud suggests, reality breaks through wish-fulfillment as time goes on, but this does not end the pull towards hallucinatory scenarios. Klein points to double aspects of hallucinatory splitting: revving up the good, erasing the bad. Whether such a state is felt to be good or bad varies. Groups and individuals tenaciously fight to maintain hallucinatory positions, disabling a full range of contact with potential difficulties: reality in the service of hallucination, rather than the reverse. Unconscious madness, rather than the challenge of channeling hallucinatory tendencies in creative social, psychological, political, aesthetic, and religious work.

The far-reaching effect of destruction by hallucinated goodness (i.e. the use of goodness to destroy or mask or obliterate destruction, to hallucinate destructiveness out of existence) is sharply noted: "Omnipotent denial of the existence of the bad object and painful situation is in the unconscious equal to annihilation by the destructive impulse" (p. 299). Denial of psychic reality, its full range of pluses and minuses, is a form of annihilation. The attempt at self-preservation (good object supporting life drive) turns against itself, falling to the temptation to blot out the death drive and annihilative tendencies. To blot out a portion of psychic reality, its ugliness and awfulness, is to preserve oneself by annihilating portions of self, psyche, the way life feels. Life drive blotting out death drive amounts to a strange victory of death indeed: good feeling in the service of obliteration.

Death drive as necessary instrument of survival perhaps, at great price. What survives is hallucinated survival, life in the service of annihilation. Relationship to others suffers deformation as connection between self and other must bear annihilative pressures it may not be able to withstand.

Klein has built an astounding nexus of interlocking operations envisioned to distribute destructive impulses throughout the psychosocial economy. Splitting, projective-introjective identifications as privileged operations of unconscious fantasy, idealization, denial of psychic reality, manic defense, omnipotent hallucinated substitution of good for bad states – all significant parts of the paranoid-schizoid position.

More can be said. Love and goodness can be split off and projected too, depleting personality, keeping it vulnerable to imaginary virtues of others. Hallucinated destruction can edge out sincerity,

devotion, love of the good, making one doubt any goodness in oneself or others or in life. Still, enough has been said to point out
Klein's emphasis on a primordial destructive gradient that runs
through psychic processes and human productions, a destructive
tendency that will not go away.

Guilt and reparation: from paranoid-schizoid to depressive positions

If Klein has a solution it has an element of tragedy, and is not a
"solution" so much as a developmental trajectory. She pictures the
infant moving from the paranoid-schizoid to the depressive position, a more mature state. The infant's use of splitting and projection is supplemented by growth of introjection and ambivalence.
The infant comes to realize the bad object it tries to attack and get rid
of, and the good object it wants are one and the same person.

The depressive elements include several components. One can
no longer uninhibitedly attack the bad and take in the good. From
this point on, good is not all good, bad is not all bad. The baby
moves from a more totalized, absolutized to a more relativized universe. Aggression is not only inhibited by fear of retaliation by a
bigger, stronger figure, but by love conjoined with guilt: one repents
injuring the good when striking the bad.

To think of self or other as all good or bad appears delusional,
hallucinatory, fantastic. Yet there is an absolutizing tendency at
work in organizing experience and Klein fingers parts of it. She
posits unconscious fantasy of all good or bad objects, their splitting,
their fusions, and the developmental task of encompassing and
integrating splits as one grows into a more differentiated, complexly
nuanced space-time world. From terrified hate expelling psychic
reality, to guilty love taking in and making room for a fuller view of
the situation. A great developmental task: making room for tensions,
conflicts and interplay of paranoid-schizoid and depressive modes
of organizing psychic life, with dominance of the latter.

The depressive position opens a field of appreciation for what the
good in another does. One feels guilty for injuring the good when
attacking the bad and seeks to make reparation. We reach a place in

infant-mother relations, where each tries to make the other feel good. Mother tries to diminish persecutory dreads in the infant and, in time, the growing baby tries to make up for its hate wishes and destructive attacks. One of Klein's great achievements is her depiction of arrays of fantasies clustering around injury and repair beginning from infancy on. Clusters of fantasy nebulae involving destruction, fear, guilt, pleasure, pain, destructive satisfactions, anxieties, agonies, and what soon enough comes to be organized as the near-ubiquitous: "I'm sorry." So much torment comes from the interplay of loving and destructive urges, wishes, fantasies.

Klein depicts an affective fantasy underpinning that plays a role in organizing schizophrenic and depressive tendencies, with many possible permutations. It almost seems in human history, in all times and places, there are two main ways of going mad, and Klein supplies some structures and contents in processes involved. The fact that paranoid-schizoid and depressive organizations are expected parts of life gives reason to view psychotic and psychotic-like processes as parts of a spectrum of experiences and behaviors. This cuts both ways. Severe clinical psychoses may involve extreme crystallizations of more widespread capacities, supporting hope for help or change. At the same time, psychotic anxieties, conflicts and operations, as intrinsic and pervasive parts of humanity, do not go away. We are challenged to become partners in development with our capacities, including ways we approach madness. We joke about there being no such thing as normalcy, that we're all mad, even normal to be mad. Klein fleshed out part of the story.

Envy and gratitude

In the later part of Klein's career, envy and gratitude became prime coordinates or expressive poles of destructive and generative tendencies (1957). While twisting her writings to stay within the Freudian (now Freudian–Kleinian mold), they, in effect, constitute a complex visionary phenomenology of polar dynamic organizations, with envy a nucleus of the "bad", gratitude a nucleus of the "good".

She placed a lot on the nursing situation as privileged example of the interplay of destructive-creative forces. It functioned at once as reality and image of a dialectic between good and bad objects coupled with inner tendencies. A central issue was whether a sense of goodness survived destructive anxieties, or whether envious attack against the good gained an upper hand. Resentment, greed, jealousy were associated with an envious core. Klein, especially, was concerned with envy's need to spoil the good breast, the good object, to denigrate the good, nourishing, enriching, creative aspects of life.

A scenario she emphasizes is whether, to what extent, an infant can experience the good in the feeding situation, and to what extent he feels the breast is selfish, holding back and keeping the best for itself. To what extent can the baby enjoy a full emotional feed, and to what extent does it feel it is missing out, getting short-changed, or that its aggressiveness is spoiling things? The baby may want inexhaustible, total fullness and spoil what goodness reality offers. Grievance vs. gratitude.

Here we have a partial clue for the origin of the current slang, "It sucks, life sucks". Sucking meaning something negative, disappointing. An eternally disappointing feed, spoiled by great expectations and destructive impulses. The expression, too, denigrates the act of sucking, dependency, helplessness, needing care – slurring a baby activity that epitomizes vulnerability and closeness. It also suggests a time before teeth, a lack of bite, oral castration. Teeth provide some power, aid digestion, but also cause pain. Problems revolving around impotence, aggression and pain are close to Klein's concerns. Earlier than genital potency, is fecundity of giving and receiving milk, image of life's nourishing aspect, associated with care, trust, faith. The arena of nourishment is also one of struggle, conflict, destruction. Can nourishment provide a context for destruction, or vice versa, or are there ever variable oscillations?

Klein depicts tensions between envious spoiling (creativity envy) and gratitude for life. We repeatedly come through attacks against the good, reform, and make use of guilt as a signal to take responsibility for destructive impacts. We learn to protect, nourish and take care of the good object within, a vital faith center. We learn to preserve a nourishing center from our attacks against it.

Klein has done something un-Nietzschean with Nietzsche. For Nietzsche, gratitude qualifies as a servile attitude, perhaps belonging with pity and resentment as part of the psychology of the weak. For Klein, gratitude is a center of strength and growth, a less paranoid ground for relationships. For Nietzsche, goodness is a trap, for Klein a primal object that supports life. Two affect-object worlds: a core of gratitude for the good vs. envious destructiveness that spoils. An inheritance from this double nucleus is a lifelong need to make use of and encompass internal divisions.

Discussion, dissension and conclusion

Klein has left a powerful legacy that puts destructiveness and love center stage. She views both as constitutional, although they vary in strength and quality for any number of inner or outer reasons. She describes vicious circles showing how attacking good objects or states intensifies mistrust and leads to further attacks. Destructive tendencies do not go away but, to some extent, can be worked with. She seems to feel that a good feed at the center of life goes a long way. Gratitude for a good internal object can lay a foundation for weathering destructive surges and anxieties, especially attacks against the good.

Winnicott (1990) does not feel the destructiveness Klein highlights need be explained by a death drive. He is closer to early Freud in seeing it as part of aliveness. Destructive and aggressive tendencies are part of life's vitality. What happens with them is the big question. Winnicott takes care to say he is not merely speaking about aggression in response to frustration, quite real in its own right. Destructive urges are an intrinsic aspect of basic aliveness and have developmental trajectories, partly depending on how they are responded to. Winnicott believes environmental trauma is crucial in personality formation, and has much to do with quality of life and relation to feelings. But if trauma helps structure aggression, it does not account for its existence in the first place. An innate aggressive capacity contributes to life in many ways.

Winnicott (1989; Eigen, 1993: Chapter 11), also, is not entirely happy with guilty reparation as a way to heal splits. He acknowledges the importance of the role of guilt in developing humane feelings. To accept responsibility and make up for destructive tendencies is part of caring. To care about injuring others is an affective core of ethical growth, a core that is violated on a daily basis.

Nevertheless, Winnicott also emphasizes how early destructive surges are responded to. Fantasies of total destruction are disconfirmed by the other's survival, filling out a sense of the realness of otherness. How the other survives attacks is crucial. Merely to retaliate, cave in or become depressed deforms or collapses the sense of other; whereas, maintaining oneself undefensively catalyzes awareness of otherness beyond fantasy control. Joy, more than guilt, characterizes this coming through.

In a similar vein, Elkin (1972) points out a reciprocity of injury: mother and child injure each other. The fact that hurt feelings are mutual mitigates the child's guilt. Something like, "After all, she hurt me too!" This does not mean there is no guilt. The guilt strand is operative too – or should be. But there are relatively guiltless threads of self and other that are part of the weave. Elkin points out the importance of forgiveness in healing splits, not just guilt (which can split one more, depending on how it functions). If a parent is not too self-justifying, insensitive, bullying and know-it-all, the child is more likely to forgive injury and remain in decent enough contact. Forgiveness rather than gratitude as a healing nucleus. But in a good circle, forgiveness and gratitude probably reinforce each other and open paths of feeling and development.

One of Bion's (1970; Eigen, 1996, 1998, 2004) differences from Klein comes from another side. He feels her paranoid-schizoid position too organized a place to start. Her infantile defenses against psychotic anxieties are not psychotic enough. Splitting-projective identification is a relatively highly structured way of dealing with originary breakdown. Bion posits an exploding O (origin, emotional reality) at the beginnings of personality, breakdown states that the evolving personality tries to encapsulate and diffuse, if not encompass. Much psycho-social life distributes psychotic breakdown, versions of madness, throughout the political, cultural, familial body, awaiting capacity for emotional digestion to evolve.

Lacan (1977, 1978) situates Klein's projective-introjective worlds in the imaginary register. Some Kleinians might situate the paranoid-schizoid position in the imaginary, and the depressive position in the symbolic. To do this justice goes beyond the limits of this chapter, but I would like to touch some nodes that bear on certain emphases in Kleinian clinical work. I would like to bring out imaginary aspects of both positions, with particular attention to imaginary threads in the depressive position.

In the Lacanian imaginary, the ego imagines itself (the subject imagines the ego) as more whole than it is, a kind of megalomanic conduit of desire, molding to fit the other's desire, desiring to capture desire, seductive, paranoid, aggressive, enslaved by influence, pretending to be master of attentional fields. Klein's depictions of splitting and projection as ways to keep a contracted ego core on top of things fits in with and amplifies Lacan's defensive, self-centered, imaginary I.

It is important to note the imaginary in the depressive position as well. On the one hand, the depressive position attempts to integrate ambivalence. Seeing the good and bad of the other, recognizing loving and destructive aspects of self. Certainly, there is growth towards reality. Nevertheless, emphasis is on valorizing and protecting an introjected good object core, particularly in face of one's destructive urges. At times, apotheosis of the good internal object gets cloying (I suspect it made Bion claustrophobic, hence his emphasis on the co-equal value of tearing apart as well as putting together; Eigen, 1986, 1993, 1996, 1998).

For Lacan, Kleinian emphasis on analyzing defenses against dependency gets too literal. Too much emphasis is placed on analyst as good object needing to be internalized and how patients spoil and destroy this need. The internal sense of wholeness and security attached to the good internal object involves an illusion reciprocal to the wholeness of the I – imaginary wholeness requiring maintenance by subterfuge.

Lacan has a mistrust for wholeness, whether of object or self. He has an inveterate fear of being suffocated by versions or fantasies of wholeness driven by unconscious desires. An extreme, perhaps paranoid view of wholeness, but also freeing.

I suspect this partly explains the moralistic, heavy-handed tone of much Kleinian literature. The patient is somehow denigrated for not making the depressive position, for remaining an ungrateful being who bites the feeding hand, a somewhat lesser being. For Lacan (an irrepressible biter), the moral superiority of a more whole being, like wholeness itself, is a signifier requiring contextual analysis.

Lacan keeps us alert as to how terms like good or whole are used by people always enmeshed in politics of desire. Psychoanalysts are not exempt. To be enslaved by goodness or wholeness is a danger Lacan rebels against. A Kleinian might want to analyze Lacan's scathing, paranoid aspect, but Lacan would try to represent symbolically the former's aim in doing so. Nevertheless, even Lacan affirms, at times, the goodness of goodness, the importance of good faith. And as his work evolved, death-work became ever more important.

Our debt to Melanie Klein is far from over. Reading her work is as eye-opening today as when I first began reading it over forty years ago. It is work that grew up in times of war. Mad destruction was a focus. She situated destructiveness in tendencies already at work in infancy, psychotic agonies at the heart of nursing at the breast, this most heart opening situation, in which a good core of feeling must work to prevail in face of annihilating elements in the total situation. She sensitizes us to momentary quivering between annihilating fantasies in tension with life-affirming ones, as well as long-term ways annihilation dread is organized. Whatever one's critique, Klein makes it impossible to bypass vulnerability to destructive fantasies, anxieties, conflicts, actions, rooted in our natures, our psycho-organisms. Her work drives home the realization that no matter how much of life's injustices we correct – and it is important we try to do so – unless we catch on to destructive forces in our very beings, our success is likely to be shaky.

CHAPTER TEN

The Annihilated Self[1]

We dream of fear of dying, corpses, threatening figures. Corpses come to life, creaking, trying to move with rusty hinges. Dead spots. Killers and rapists threaten to overpower us in dreams. Fear of being overpowered permeates psychic life.

I don't think any of us survive infancy or childhood fully alive. What lives survives on graves of self that didn't make it. We leave a lot behind to be what we are now, to be what we can be.

We cover not only nakedness but annihilation. We try to look better than we are, more alive, more appealing. We try to mask a sense of an annihilated self with signs of life.

* * *

Marlene speaks about someone who wears tons of make-up to hide her scary, broken face. Emboldened by their contact and driven by need, this person comes in one day without make-up and shows herself as she is. Chilling, bloodcurdling, necessary. She shows her ravaged self to the one person who can take it. No, incorrect. Marlene may not be able to take it. She shows herself whether or not Marlene can take it. That is closer. To risk in therapy what no one can take. The human race has not evolved capacity to take what it does to itself, the pain people inflict on each other. In therapy one risks what is too much for another, too much for oneself. One risks what no one can take or may ever be able to take. *That* enters the room and is shared, whether or not anyone can take it.

*   *   *

A sharing of what can't be taken, the full scope of her patient's annihilation. Marlene feels it in cringing at the sight of her patient's unveiled face, a ghastly horror myths sometimes portray. Unbearable – how could this happen to a human being?!

She passes it to us. We join the community of those who speak about such things and express them in art. The most usual form of expression is transmission of trauma, passing trauma on to someone else, the next generation, those close to one. Inflicting ghastly things on life, through politics, family, intimacy, war, economic mendacity.

Therapy takes time to sense and see what we do to each other. It dwells with impacts, sharing innermost ravage. A coming out, a showing. Even if the annihilated face pierces Marlene, stops her cold, it has been registered, noted. That Marlene is done in by what can not be sustained enables the patient to make her mark, her impact. A glimpse of the worst puts the other out of play, but the other continues, therapy continues. In the context of therapy, derailment is a kind of sharing, a sharing of being put out of play.

*   *   *

In the case that Marlene is impelled to share, a glimpse of the whole is compressed in a face. A face that is usually covered, hidden. It is shameful to look like the annihilated being one is. It would turn others off, make one even more alone. Yet Marlene's patient is driven to do just this. It is something therapy invites, even propels. Again, it is not a matter of surviving what can't be survived but sharing annihilation. Being annihilated together. Her patient's inmost devastation breaks into another human being, more thoroughly than a thief breaking into a dream.

*   *   *

An aside on Oedipus piercing his eyes, blinding himself. There are references in myth, religion, literature of dying, turning to stone, salt, some paralyzing consequence, by seeing what can't be seen or shouldn't be seen. That you can't see God and live or see Medusa's face directly and live are among images that express the sense of being done in by too much, by not being up to experience, the intensity of impact. Likewise, Oedipus.

It is not simply that he blinded himself out of guilt or shame (a pars pro toto parallel of Jocasta's suicide), but that seeing is blinding. Staring directly into the soul, like staring directly at the sun, can be too much for the organ of sight, or the capacity for experiencing. A theme of psychoanalysis: we can not take, do not take well, do not know what to do with the ways psyche works. Yet we are drawn to see what blinds us.

One of the Bible stories touching this is Aaron's sons burnt to a crisp trying to get too close to God in their own way. They made "strange" sacrifice. Strange or weird can mean singular, individual, own. My own last name, Eigen, unites such nuances in its history, meaning strange, weird, individual, common, proper, own.

Aaron's sons did not follow the prescribed laws of sacrifice. They invented their own ritual, followed their own prompting. Rabbinic commentary says they tried to get to God directly, like the tower of Babel, an assault on divinity, an attempt at appropriation. Mystical Judaism says they burned with desire to be close to God, consuming desire. Consumed by desire, a fire that leaves nothing but God, openness, *sunyata*.

That coming to grips with ourselves is damaging is an old theme. An equally old theme is that not coming to grips with ourselves is damaging. We have made a notation. Damage is part of life processes and the emergence of psychic life, symbolic life, ushers in new kinds of damage. Damage to personality, self, feeling, ego, spirit – new kinds of pain we create with each other.

* * *

Many of us want to let psychic reality speak, let experience speak, create something together. An urge to jump in, pull threads, mess up, muck around, let develop what wants to develop. In this discussion we are headed for the annihilated self. Marlene's patient's real face as frightening, bloodcurdling takes us straight to the place we are headed.

We carry around an annihilated self. It can be seen peeking out in this or that trait or expression. Marlene's patient risks showing it in a moment of truth. At times it is seen as a center of the emotive perceptual field. I think many of us see each other's annihilated self. Like hounds, we sniff it out. Even if we look OK, we can x-ray

in, find it. We begin to train ourselves to stick with what is strangulated, gone. There is no one way to talk about this. Words like "the"
or "a" – *the* annihilated self – seem to reify, freeze a process. But they
call attention to something that needs attending.

I can envision a time when each other's annihilated self will be
known, felt, accepted. I don't mean known as scientifically known,
all parts laid out. We may or may not know all the details about
our annihilated selves. But we know such things exist, even if we
don't know what to say of them. Annihilation processes are part
of the way we are constituted. We live with dead areas. My hope is
that making room for our annihilated self will enable us to be less
destructive. We often injure, even destroy each other, in order to reach
the realness of our annihilated beings. How much destructiveness
aims at "showing" how destroyed we feel! Therapy is one place to
try to contact the annihilated self without destroying ourselves.
Speaking, sensing and imagining is a less costly method of discovery
than giving in to the compulsion to destroy.

*   *   *

Ellen speaks about the annihilated self in eating disorders and refers
to a catastrophe at the beginning of personality formation. A patient
dreamt she had been chopped into multiple parts by her mother
and was in a bathtub full of blood. Ellen thought of a Soprano's
episode too frightening for her to watch. Her patient depicted a
psychic reality too awful to take in, yet therapy drew it out in a
dream.

Ellen (Pearlman, 2005) has worked with eating disorders for
many years and knows the territory. She says, "My feeling is that
most eating disorder patients are grossed out by their bodies top to
bottom and that they often have bottom and top confused, orifices
are interchangeable. They chop their bodies up and will find one
part that is acceptable. I had one patient who loved her feet, but
couldn't see any of the rest of her body. I have one patient who has a
tummy/mind confusion. When she eats and feels the food stay too
long, she fears she will go crazy, a reversal of when she was left too
long in the crib without food or attention. Neither psychic digestion
nor body digestion can be trusted."

These individuals create a sense of devastation in their bodies,
expressing with part of themselves a more total sense of annihilation. The ravaged, traumatized, annihilated self or self aspects find

expression by channeling a circumscribed function. Although "food disorders" may present themselves as limited (pars pro toto), they can lead to death, duped by their own unconscious logic.

* * *

Another day Ellen tells of dread she felt upon seeing a bald woman in her exercise class, with one breast clearly delineated in her t-shirt. "Even having been through the same experience, I found it hard to know how to respond. I admired her bravery, but also knew it could be overcompensation. I have never gone in public, outside my family, without my prosthesis. I wanted to wish her well, tell her I'd been there, but didn't want to be reminded of it either. Finally, I did just see her, didn't avert my eyes, wasn't embarrassed for her. Before my cancer experience I probably wouldn't have felt that way. I wouldn't have been able to do that. That's something . . ."

The chill Marlene felt when her patient unmasked her horrific face brought Marlene back to her mastectomy, the loss, rupture, disfigurement. Profound dread runs through her body. Her patient's face is her body. Her dismembered body radiates further back to childhood dreams of corpses, dying bodies, ghastly terrors, numb terrors, blank terrors. Dream terrors disfigure our beings, portray the way disfigurement feels.

Ellen and Marlene share backlogs of childhood terror and trauma of adult disease. Pain makes us hide. So much shame is attached to pain. We think pain is only private and withdraw. So much childhood pain goes unanswered or misunderstood. People are afraid of each other's pain and their own, helpless, not knowing how to respond to the pain of life. Yet pain resonates, links. To some extent, we grow into it and it becomes part of our sense of community, part of reaching out. Ellen and Marlene share coming through, fear of not coming through, pressure to transform. We would rather not have to grow this way. But in their case, struggle opens pathways.

* * *

Marlene speaks of a childhood dream. "The background of the dream was an absolute, devastating, horrific silence. On a beach lay dozens of corpses, their motionlessness melded into the silence and steeped it with death. Or perhaps I should say that death showed itself in the terrifying amalgam of silence, dead bodies, and motionlessness. The sensations of the dream I can still feel today when I remember it, although I have not remembered it in years, until this seminar. I felt I never quite understood it. It did not seem to fit in with traditional interpretations. Now I see that this dream was my annihilated self. The self my patient was threatening to re-evoke in me and from which I so wanted to run. It was the self that I faced with breast cancer and mastectomy. I believe I can go into my sessions with a bit more understanding, in a felt way, with having in dream and in words what I am so afraid of facing in her ghastly, blood curdling annihilated self."

Ellen and Marlene were able to see the unseeable, stay with the unstayable. A little more. Their work, their persons, better for it.

Part of this seeing and staying involves letting death be. Marlene's corpses, annihilated self, threat of actual as well as psychic death and deformation, her patient's devastated face, devastated soul: one does not breathe life into death nor undertake reparative or hysterical activity to make life happen. One dies in some ways. Marlene stays with it, tastes it, awakened to the fact that she can let deadness be. Then the next thing happens, a process emerges, continues. We embolden each other to stay with what needs to be noticed. Our interactions play a role in letting this happen, e.g. Marlene's patient's need to show the truth of her horror. We need to show what is too horrible to be seen. Even if we see it, we would not know what to do with it.

A patient told me no one in her family knew what to do with a baby. She kept herself in life by relating to God. She developed an intense connection to God and masturbated a lot. When she got older she lived out some eros with men, never enough. A whole middle section of her life was never born sufficiently or died. She saw the middle area in dreams of corpses, felt dead spots, blank spots in her body. She spoke with spiritual and erotic intensity but something in between was missing. The two extremes filled a hiatus, pouring spirit and eros into a vacuum.

A lot of effort is spent trying not to look dead or trying not to see the deadness. Many deflect it into wars or disastrous triumphs of one or another sort, in which corpses litter the psychic landscape and the outside world (no neat division here). We create disasters as an attempt to make our sense of being damaged seen. Our damaged selves damage the world as a form of self-expression. Some years ago, a tour guide in the Florida everglades spoke of the dying of the waters. One wonders what it takes to be seen.

I vividly feel something of what Ellen expresses, seeing breast/ no-breast baldness, bald lack showing itself like Marlene's patient's devastated face. Recoil, implicit horror, revulsion, or whatever fits the feeling, perhaps a kind of horrific awe. There are moments when a baby sees the Medusa mother's face. Or a devil face, a fiend. I am not sure a baby sees death. If a baby sees death it is an animated death, all the more frightening in being alive. Seeing death's face, then, a certain kind of death. Shock, tightening, freezing, screaming and, if not comforted, dying out. There is already a partial dying out in the state of shock, the shock of the aw-ful. One can not believe even at an early age such things can happen, such things are happening to one. A shock going on all life long. Sometimes it seems worse in the teens or twenties because of the particular level of self-consciousness achieved. It is dangerous to think that shock lessens with age: I am familiar with older persons dying from shock. We are never out of the woods on this score.

We are only partly restored when we are restored. We know this because sometimes we feel more fully restored or reach a new dimension of living, and feel the difference. Ellen and Marlene struggled profoundly to meet the tragic and come through, to the point where things fell into place, reality became reality once more, just so, as it is, more fully so, more textured, the richly scarred self opening portals. Marlene (Goldsmith, 2004) speaks of her paper on Frida Kahlo's journey into body pain, soul agony, art. She endures being twisted beyond recognition yet ends by saying, "Vive la vida".

* * *

Jeff's childhood dream: "I'm at the beach looking out at the ocean. A boat approaches. I know that when the boat reaches the shore, if I get on it, I will die. It is a death boat coming to ferry me to some place called Death. I woke up screaming. My parents tell me all I talked about was 'the boat-man' for the next several weeks. They didn't know what I was talking about. I didn't know, consciously, what I was talking about. I grew up on Puget Sound. But I wasn't talking about boats. I was trying to talk about death, or, the preconception of death. Why? As an adult I think it was because my father's father died just a few weeks before I was born. I know my father wanted his father to see me. My father's mother died a year after I was born. I'm named after my mother's father who died when she was 12. My mother worried that I would die as a baby, once rushed me to the hospital to have my stomach pumped because she didn't know whether or not I'd eaten dirt in the yard that had slug poison in it. My sister almost died as a fetus and her teens were filled with black and poison fragments of self and object fusing, intruding and gnawing and exploding. Something must happen in the baby's mind and body to process 'the family atmosphere' and death was part of the mix in mine and so that became part of the depression, psychosomatic direction, and need to use imagination to find ways of moving through agonies. Intensity was the most frightening. But somehow one grows."

Jeff carves out a history for the fear of death, for the particular forms death takes in *his* life. But there is no history for death itself. Death or consciousness of death propels history. Death provides a history of depression. Death and fear of death seep through Jeff's family. In the dream, death is compressed. The death boat, the boat-man: death so often depicted as movement, passage. A movement that stills movement.

The boatman of the River Styx, Rimbaud's drunken boat, meeting Death in the Upanishads . . . blends of trauma and beauty, annihilation and creativity. Children have a drive to know death as well as sex. A drive towards the real, to experience with all their might, a drive that is frightened out of them, depressed out of them. The boat-man scares the life out of them. Areas of deadness, emptiness ensue. One becomes frightened of life. The dream teaches that children get more than they bargained for. They get the knowledge they were after and *that* petrifies them.

It is not just the turning back but the *seeing* of destruction, the destructive truth, that turns Lot's wife to salt. And Orpheus? Is it merely because he turns to see Eurydice that he loses her, or because seeing is too much, the hell that touches her too much to bear?

Yet there is need for intensity, immersion, resistance, impact. As well as need to hide and make believe things are better and need to go on. A drive to know what one is afraid to know, taste what one is afraid to taste. The boat as death driven body, a body one feels is life. For Rimbaud, the boat adrift in life is poetic impulse, psychic movement. Some fear psychic movement as death. The body lets one down, life lets one down. To go on, drive through everything that slows one up, to move forward with gunshot in one's gut, a hole in one's heart. One gains a sense of satisfaction moving with such impediments, sometimes racing, flying. No wonder we can't get out of bed. We appreciate the Zen master who lifts a finger: if you can lift a finger, you can do anything.

To lift oneself up, get a lift, lighten spirit. We must be quite a weight to ourselves.

Jeff's aesthetic and truth sense is part of innate reality. Over a lifetime it gains intensity, fills out by tasting death. Jeff says death shut him down, provoked fear of intensity. He has written about deep mind-destructive processes (Eaton, 2005). What puts one out of play when one is younger feeds one's unfolding as one grows. One contracts with threats for many years. Chilled with terror, fearful of unending contraction. But as a grown-up, life grows larger, taking death in. One grows into death. Death warms life as one grows into it, adds tone to beauty, although this doesn't stop us from screaming. "I woke up screaming." As a child, as an adult. A scream we never grow into completely.

* * *

Mac: "One day many years ago I was watching the morning news and saw JonBenet Ramsey for the first time. Performing. As accompaniment to the news of her murder. (I knew nothing of child beauty pageants.) I found myself dissolved in tears. 'How could anyone do that to a child?' I asked myself – sexualize a child in that way and parade that to a pedophilic culture. The image of that child entered my psyche the way a traumatic image must. All defenses were stripped away. The psyche was reduced to sufferance. A suffering that wouldn't stop, uncontainable suffering. For me the only possible response was to try to constitute her trauma, to let her speak. Three years later I had a play with her as the main character: only one who doesn't die at 6 but who we meet at 35 in a series of monologues interspersed with flashbacks (Davis, 2003). The brunt of it all was not to resolve her trauma but to constitute it. To try to get inside a psyche that was so deeply violated that consciousness itself became the agony of the why, to open to the traumatic wound at the core of the psyche and living from there."

Mac speaks of tragic creativity growing from this pain, this agony at the heart of psychic trauma. Art, words growing from violation, annihilation. One constitutes oneself within this annihilated core.

He shares a dream from his own childhood: "Still a child,

dressed in the little blue Navy suit modeled on the one my father wore, I lie in a casket in a dim room lighted only by candles. All the family is there, hushed, seated in a circle, like mannequins frozen in formal poses and ritual gestures. I am calm (perhaps for the first time). All struggle is gone, all protest. I accept what has happened in a spirit of love. Only one thing remains. A request. Without moving I ask them to make an exception to a rule that I already know cannot be broken. But it is the thing I need more than anything. And so I ask them again to bring Brownie, the teddy bear I love, and place him next to me so I won't be alone. It is a plea but there is no panic in it, yet no hope that it will be heeded. And so finally in the great rush of what must be love I accept it all. It is what they've been waiting for, the thing that enables them to cry. The cry grows. It is the bond that unites them, giving them the identity they need to be a family. This knowledge is the central reality that frees me to what I now know I must do . . . I'm alone then, down in a crypt, in a cold stone place, a realm of shadow in a dim twilight. I go forward, toward a casket. I see myself lying there, in it – and I become what I see. A child is sleeping, beautiful and resigned. The beginnings of a smile are frozen on his lips. But no one will come to kiss them back to life. He will stay like this forever. He is sleeping but he will not awaken."

Among Mac's remarks: "My hunch is that if we get to the annihilated self we will find a dead child. That dead child is, of course, oneself."

One reason I write is so I do not entirely remain a resigned sleeping beauty at whom I stare while the Greek chorus of my stiffened soul weeps. You can see why love can be mistrusted. It keeps one quiet. It creates a bond of death. Beautiful resignation. Look what one has to do to bring the family together: one has to die to keep the family together, a death that is part of socialization. A toxic bond, a damaged bond acting as personal and social cement. The dream expresses a dying out or mock death that goads Mac to speak. Keep the family together, no matter how impossible. Keep the self together, no matter how impossible. We are speaking of existential nuclei, inner dead babies, or almost dead babies, or pretend death. This is a precious transmission.

Love as an awful force to keep one down. Mac is telling us he refuses to be quiet. He will not go through his whole life watching the death of himself, a ghost of himself, a sleeping beauty akin to the mysterious resignation of Peter Pan's mother (in Barrie's prose).

In *Toxic Nourishment* (1999: 150–4) I described a man falling into passive inertia, yet listening, listening. For the sound of his parents in the dark? For signs of his dying process? We listen for signs of life and for signs of un-life. Mac objects to "normalcy" not only as masking psychosis but as a form of madness. One is stuffed with deforming socialization processes that one takes a stand over and against as one goes under.

We see in this seminar waves of the annihilated self, hints of processes. Many people communicate the reality of some kind of dying or devastation. A seemingly cellular infiltration of the self by psychic death is meaningful. There is hunger to share it.

Psychic death, even more than physical death, is complex. Psychic death is woven with many threads of life and simulacra of life. Death feeds death with sparks of life. Even pretend life is not without the nerves of life. Where there is exploitation and subterfuge someone pays with some sort of life loss. The powerful self and the annihilated self are aspects of life, aspects of *our* lives.

It was moving that people shared the sense of devastation related to body, to face, to children, to family. One might say Annihilation with a Thousand Faces, but it is more than 1000. We are not celebrating trauma but constituting it, attesting to its reality. Why? Many reasons, one being that trauma and its effects get brainwashed, twisted, whitewashed, blackwashed away.

We can see on the political scene how adults con children, infiltrate minds, twist reality. We were fed lies to go to war in Iraq (note an implicit infant-breast reference), fed catastrophic threats (*they* have weapons of mass destruction). Catastrophic anxiety is manipulated in the service of power and control, exploited as part of "socialization" processes. We fuzz out our sense of taking in lies, anesthetize disbelief as we give in. Leaders play on fear of destruction to get people to destroy, play on trauma to channel the will to traumatize, manipulate ideals to get people to do what they want. Leaders pretend to know what they are doing and we dull our awareness that they are quasi-delusional. We join in our leaders' hallucinations (and in hallucinating leaders) in our need to channel psychotic dreads by exercising power.

What I feel happening in communication attempts in this seminar is making room for the annihilated self and annihilating processes, in the hope that we will not have to damage each other too badly. We are trying to share what we are up against, touch it, taste it. Sensitivity to this "ouch" is important. Often it tells us something bad is happening. Not only bad but wrong, evil. A sensitivity implicitly allied with a sense of justice, a justice that cares for human beings. Mac's shattering pain that he will never recover from upon seeing JonBenet's disfigurement on the altar of familial and social narcissism bears witness to a link between the impact of trauma on sensitivity and potential ethics. Too often, instead of authentic ethical concern, waves of derangement fill the space where sensitivity to trauma ought to be. An ethical imperative worth thinking about, akin to the golden rule, based on sensitivity to trauma, an ethical impulse we bury in shame, fear, powerlessness, and the will to power. Our job is to help sensitivity to evolve, which includes recovering and developing the ethical impulse nested in it.

*   *   *

Is there a particular way to approach the annihilated self? In talks one is often asked, "How do you do it? What should I do?" There is no one way. Here is a short recounting of a father linking with a son's sense of death. In this case, death was a concrete childhood threat, not exactly the annihilated self we are speaking of (self crushed through trauma and growth). However, the method of approach is related to what we are trying to connect with.

Kerry (for more from this speaker, see Gordon, 2004): "When my youngest son was three months old, he developed a rare disease that should have killed him (by all odds) and almost did kill him. He spent three years on chemotherapy, and twice more was at the threshold of death. There are, of course, family stories about this, but he has been vigorously healthy now for many years and this experience is not often (overtly) in the foreground any more. From about five years of age on, sometimes with external cues and sometimes not, he would suddenly collapse into a place of abject horror and say to me 'Daddy, I don't want to die'. (At 14, this is now about the only time he says 'Daddy'.) I very quickly learned that 'comforting' him was not only useless, but in fact made it worse. For years now, when this happens I find myself collapsing with him, feeling a kind of . . . something . . . which I will not even try to name. I nod and we will make some kind of light physical contact and within a few seemingly endless moments it will pass for both of us. Over the last couple of years the statement has changed to 'Daddy, I'm going to die', offered matter-of-factly in tone, but with a look that is, once again, something I can't describe. It feels so true to me that this felt awareness of the horizon line of life/death (I have a fantasy that he feels death at a cellular level) is one of the (many) wavelengths of experience which combine to create his being.

"I can't say that what I provide him in these moments is so much containment as it is company, or maybe containment through company. Which brings me to a question asked earlier: why we sometimes devastate others, maybe most particularly those we love the most. I have a strong sense that we often do it because our most broken, most annihilated selves crave companionship, and we really don't know what else to do."

This collapse into being with another, the deepest states of the other – isn't this something of the kind of sensitivity that gives our annihilated states a home?

Note

1. This chapter draws on a PsyBc online seminar I gave in May 2005, "Faith and Destructiveness". The seminar was based on two readings, "Killers in Dreams" (Chapter 7 in *Emotional Storm*, 2005) and "A Basic Rhythm" (Chapter 2 in *The Sensitive Self*, 2004). My concern was to bring out viral aspects of our psychic life and ways we interact with them. An important thread that emerged clustered around "the annihilated self", a theme that spontaneously grew out of the postings. I have brought some of the postings together here and let them play off each other, adding to, enriching, complicating our need to meet and make room for our annihilated selves. The people I quote gave full permission to use their postings.

POSTSCRIPT

F eelings matter.
Feeling matters.
Soldiers are surprised by what war does to them. A colleague recently told me about another (how many I've heard about!) Vietnam veteran who hung himself, a man who went berserk and coldly killed a field of men exposed to his helicopter fire, seeking revenge for a buddy who had been killed. Do you think this an odd juxtaposition: to go berserk and coldly kill? To be cold and mad? They seem like opposites but they are not. When it comes to violence, they often fuse.

This young man could not bear the fact that he survived and his buddy didn't. What gave him permission to mow down a field of youths? He described many of them as tall, strong, solid. They did not look like villains. They shone with life. His commander knew what he was doing. In his national unconscious, he was being patriotic, justified, if not exactly doing the right thing, then doing the wrong thing for a bigger right, the right thing in war. Guilt never left. It grew with years, corroding his spirit, eroding life.

We like to think we can get away with things. We think we can just because we do get away with them a good part of the time. We

see other people who get away with even more. We see some who
obviously pay a price and others we don't know about. We only
imagine.

I believe we are all paying a price for the way our society is
structured. Today a special line of force involves the way corporate
power influences how feelings are felt. Media, assisted by techno-
logy that penetrates our emotional veins, organizes what can and can
not be experienced or, at least, favors certain modes of interpretation
of experience over others. So-called free-market competitiveness,
has a certain monotheism at its base: the worship of money, whether
fused with pleasure or power. Power is its own kind of pleasure. The
power of power gives one a high that is hard to penetrate, a kind of
shield around life, until the shield cracks.

I think one reason people come to therapy is to say feelings do
matter. It matters to be a feeling person. At this juncture, there are
few places to learn how to grow in this fashion. Power channels
feelings into lines of force that work for it. But feelings are messier
and try to escape. To breathe psychically requires more than power
structures allow. Neither tyranny of left nor right does justice to the
life of feeling.

The chapters in this book give the life of feeling a voice. There is
a level or dimension of being in which voice resonates with voice.
All voices are multi-toned. Practicality may force us into one line
of sound over another. But we hear other voices, other parts of our
voice. We need places where we can let them play, hear each other,
seek birth nuances. There is a hunger for nuance, for psychic taste.
We taste each other's psyches and have a drive to do something
good with this special form of play, this precious kind of taste.

Too often power simulates play, channels feelings in deadly earn-
est into what sells or dominates, takes the play out of feelings, culti-
vates violence and inertia, corrupts play. Power is part of life, part
of vitality. Creative power, ethical power, the power of goodness –
voices rich in their own ways. We do not know if there are viable
alternatives to exploitative, predatory power or if the latter can be
"exploited" for better use. We do not know to what extent we can tilt
our beings towards less toxic use of power. We do not even know to
what extent we can try.

Yet individuals do try, in their own private struggles and in the
larger social sphere. We see in the depths of private lives forces that

get magnified in the larger world, and in our secret beings we find magnified hints of forces that go undetected in the social sphere. Social reform is not enough without working with the human psyche that informs the ways we govern ourselves. We need to work both ends at once, private and public, since they are part of one fabric.

REFERENCES

Abraham, K. (1973). *Selected Papers*. London: Hogarth Press.

Bion, W. R. (1962). *Learning From Experience*. London: Karnac Books (1984).

Bion, W. R. (1970). *Attention and Interpretation*. London: Karnac Books (1984).

Bion, W. R. (1992). *Cogitations*. London: Karnac Books.

Davis, W. A. (2003). An Evening with JonBenet Ramsey: A Play and Two Essays. Xlibris Corporation.

Eaton, J. L. (2005). The obstructive object. *The Psychoanalytic Review, 92*: 355–372.

Eigen, M. (1986). *The Psychotic Core*. London: Karnac Books (2004).

Eigen, M. (1993). *The Electrified Tightrope*, A. Phillips (Ed.). London: Karnac Books (2004).

Eigen, M. (1996). *Psychic Deadness*. London: Karnac Books (2004).

Eigen, M. (1998). *The Psychoanalytic Mystic*. London: Free Association Books.

Eigen, M. (1999). *Toxic Nourishment*. London: Karnac Books.

Eigen, M. (2001). *Damaged Bonds*. London: Karnac Books.

Eigen, M. (2004). *The Sensitive Self*. Middletown, CT: Wesleyan University Press.

Eigen, M. (2005). *Emotional Storm*. Middletown, CT: Wesleyan University Press.

Elkin, H. (1972). On selfhood and the development of ego structures in infancy. *The Psychoanalytic Review, 59*: 389–416.

Ferenczi, S. (1955). *The Selected Papers of Sandor Ferenczi, M.D: Problems and Methods of Psychoanalysis, Vol. 3*. New York: Basic Books.

Freud, S. (1911). Psychoanalytic notes on an autobiographical account of a case of paranoia (dementia paranoides). *Standard Edition 12*: 3–82.

Freud, S. (1920). Beyond the pleasure principle. *Standard Edition, 18*: 1–64.

Freud, S. (1921). Group psychology and the analysis of the Ego. *Standard Edition, 18*: 65–143.

Freud, S. (1937). Analysis terminable and interminable. *Standard Edition, 23*: 216–253.

Freud, S. (1940). An outline of psycho-analysis. *Standard Edition, 23*: 141–207.

Ghent, E. (1990). Masochism, submission, surrender: Masochism as a perversion of surrender. *Contemporary Psychoanalysis, 26*: 108–136.

Goldsmith, M. (2004). Frida Kahlo: Abjection, psychic deadness, and the creative impulse. *The Psychoanalytic Review, 91*: 723–758.

Gordon, K. (2004). The tiger's stripe: Some thoughts on psychoanalysis, gnosis, and the experience of wonderment. *Contemporary Psychoanalysis, 40*: 5–45.

Klein, M. (1946). Notes on some schizoid mechanisms. In: M. Klein, P. Heimann, S. Isaacs, & J. Riviere (Eds), *Developments in Psychoanalysis*. London: Hogarth Press (1952), pp. 292–320.

Klein, M. (1957). *Envy and Gratitude*. New York: Basic Books.

Lacan, J. (1977). *Ecrits*. A. Sheridan (Trans.). New York: Norton.

Lacan, J. (1978). *The Four Fundamental Concepts of Psychoanalysis*, J.-A. Miller (Ed.) & A. Sheridan (Trans.). New York: Norton.

Levinas, E. (1969). *Totality and Infinity*, A. Lingis (Trans.). Pittsburgh: Duquesne University Press.

Milner, M. (1969). *The Hands of the Living God*. New York: International Universities Press.

Pearlman, E. (2005). Terror of desire: The etiology of eating disorders from an attachment theory perspective. *The Psychoanalytic Review, 92*: 223–336.

Winnicott, D. W. (1965). *The Maturational Processes and the Facilitating Environment*. London: Karnac Books (1990).

Winnicott, D. W. (1988/1990). *Human Nature*. New York: Schocken Books.

Winnicott, D. W. (1989/1992). *Psychoanalytic Explorations*, C. Winnicott, R. Shepherd, and M. Davis (Eds). Cambridge, MA: Harvard University Press.

INDEX